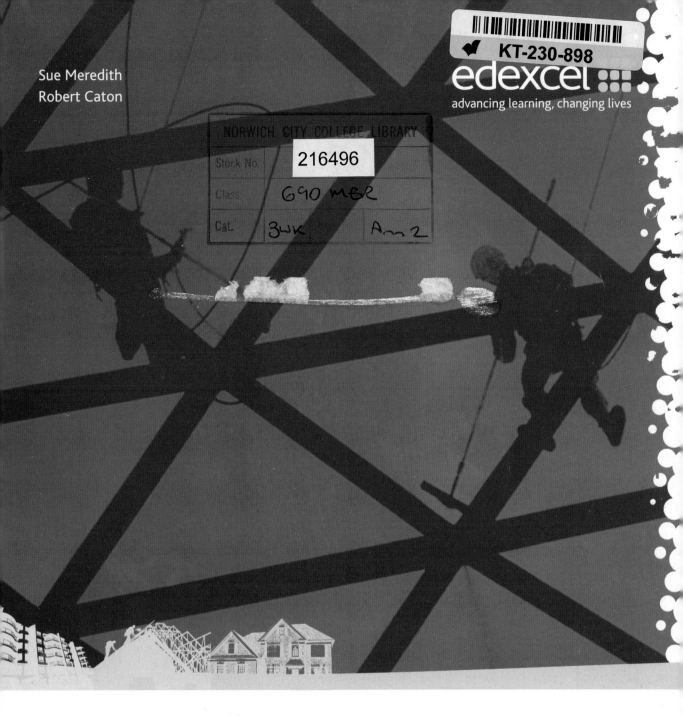

Sue Meredith
Robert Caton

edexcel
advancing learning, changing lives

Edexcel Diploma

Construction and the Built Environment

Level 1 Foundation

216 496

Published by
Pearson Education
Edinburgh Gate
Harlow
Essex
CM20 2JE

ISBN: 978-0-43550-043-6

Illustrations by Oxford Designers & Illustrators
Picture research by Thelma Gilbert
Index by Richard Howard
Designed and typeset by Steve Moulds, DSM Partnership
Printed and bound by Graficas Estella, Bilboa, Spain

Acknowledgements
Thanks to Paul Cleary for his links with the Construction professionals featured in this book.

The publisher would like to thank the following for their kind permission to reproduce their photographs:

(key: b-bottom; c-centre; l-left; r-right; t-top)

0800Handyman: 173; **Alamy Images**: Peter Adam Photography 8; Andrew Ammendolia 79; Graham Bell 125; Mark Boulton 39r; Bubbles Photography 171; Domonic Burke 41; Ashley Cooper 12b; Sylvia Cordaiy 178–9; Bob Croxford 180; Gregory Davies 38; Paul Doyle 87; Clynt Garnham 191; Shaun Higson 12t; David Hoffman 16; Chris Howes 141, 152–3, 155; ICP 199; ImageState 145; Natural History Museum 39l; Anthony Nettle 94–5; PCL 37; Picturesofeurope 133; Ted Pink 162; Donald Pye 34–5; Chris Rose 122–3; Chas Spadbery 62; Victor Watts 60–61; Woodystock 55; **Diane Auckland**: 119; **Choochoos Day Nursery**: 147; **Construction Photography**: 65, 96, 160, 166, 168, 196; **Corbis**: 68b, 117, 128l; **Corus Living Solutions**: 201; Tim Crocker: 30; **Ecoscene**: 136; **Robert Harding World Imagery**: 70; **Stephen Manley**: 180, 197; **No Credit**: 89; **Offsitesolutions**: 99; **PA Photos**: 6–7, 134; **PRP Architects**: 57; Rex Features: 22, 128r, 130; **Science Photo Library Ltd**: 72; **Screwfix**: 25b, 67 (boots), 67 (ear defenders), 67 (goggles), 67 (hat), 67 (mask); **Roger Scruton**: 14, 25, 29, 68t, 103, 138, 188; **Skyscan Photolibrary**: 18; **Suffolk Housing Society**: 104; **Troup Bywaters & Anders**: 9

Cover images: *Front*: Denise Lyons

Contents

About this book

Congratulations on your decision to take Edexcel's Foundation Diploma in Construction and the Built Environment! This book will help you in all seven units of your course, providing opportunities to develop functional skills, Personal, Learning and Thinking Skills, and to learn about the world of work.

There is a chapter devoted to every unit, and each chapter opens with the following:

» Overview – a description of what is covered in the unit

» Skills list – a checklist of the skills covered in the unit

» Job watch – a list of relevant careers

This book contains many features that will help you relate your learning to the workplace and assist you in making links to other parts of the Diploma.

» Margin notes provide interesting facts and get you thinking about the industry.

FIND OUT

There is an Approved Code of Practice (ACoP) for the CDM regulations that gives practical advice for all those involved in construction work on how to comply with the law. Find out more about this at: http://www.hse.gov.uk/construction/cdm/acop.htm

CHECK IT OUT

The National Heritage Training Group is committed to sustaining traditional skills for the maintenance of heritage properties.
Find out more about these traditional skills by visiting the following website:

http://www.nhtg.org.uk/heritageIndex.asp

TRY THIS

Quarried rock, such as limestone, is used in a variety of different ways in construction. Have a look at the house on this website, which shows you how stone products are used:

http://www.tarmac.co.uk/quarryville/stoneSt/house.html

DID YOU KNOW?

Reclamation yards specialise in recovering 'architectural effects' such as flagstones, oak beams, fireplaces, stone mullion window surrounds, cast iron drainpipes, gutters and hoppers and selling them to property owners seeking authentic detail to add to period properties.

» Activities link directly to Personal, Learning and Thinking Skills and functional skills – all an important part of passing your course and vital for your future career.

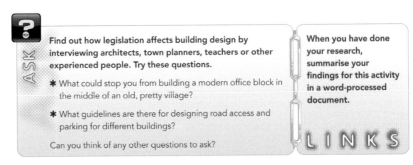

ASK

Find out how legislation affects building design by interviewing architects, town planners, teachers or other experienced people. Try these questions.

* What could stop you from building a modern office block in the middle of an old, pretty village?

* What guidelines are there for designing road access and parking for different buildings?

Can you think of any other questions to ask?

When you have done your research, summarise your findings for this activity in a word-processed document.

LINKS

» @work activities help you to think about how your learning could
be applied during your work placement.

Conduct an inventory of the tools and equipment used in
your work experience workplace for the craft area that you
work in. This may involve asking an experienced worker to
show you and discuss with you the content of their toolbox.
Find out how often the tools are replaced and how each
tool is maintained.

» Site visit features provide a snapshot of real issues in the
workplace.

» 'I want to be…' lets you hear from real people what it is like to
work in the Construction industry.

Each chapter ends with assessment tips and an opportunity for you
to check your skills and summarise what you've learned. You can
also find help with technical terms in the glossary on p. 204.

We hope you enjoy using this book, and we wish you the very best
for your Diploma course and your future career in Construction and
the Built Environment.

OVERVIEW

The construction industry provides places for us all to live, work and learn as well as **infrastructure** such as roads, power stations, airports and railways. All construction has an effect on its surroundings and it is important that new buildings and other structures are designed to have the smallest possible negative impact on the natural environment – something that was not always the case in the past. Construction designs are produced by architects, town planners, or building services engineers, and it is an important part of their job to make sure that structures provide a healthy and pleasant environment for their users and fit in with the natural surroundings. A successful designer in the construction industry will make sure that every building or structure design will:

» fit the client's **specification**

» suit the intended use

» be pleasing to the eye

» be approved by the local community

» blend with the local built environment

» have a minimal impact on the natural environment

» use **sustainable** materials and methods.

This unit will also help you to understand how the planning process works and how planning impacts on construction design. You will find out about the different types of construction materials available and how to choose the most suitable and cost-effective material for each part of a construction design. For instance, high-strength steel might be the best material for a structure bearing a great load, but a timber frame would better suit a single-storey building. It is important to keep up-to-date with new developments in technology, materials and construction techniques so that your designs and structures are always the very best they can be.

Design the Built Environment: Design Influences

Skills list

At the end of this unit, you should:

» know how designs are influenced by human and physical factors

» understand the basic need for planning

» understand the basic need for sustainability and environmental protection

» be able to describe the properties and uses of typical construction materials.

Job watch

Job roles that involve design and planning skills in the construction industry include:

» architect
» architectural technician
» structural engineer
» building services engineer
» civil engineer
» surveyor
» town planner
» landscape architect.

The influence of human and physical factors on design

For each new building, the designer must look very carefully at the place where the building is to be constructed and assess the impact of each aspect of the design on that location. You need to ask questions such as:

» How old are the surrounding buildings and what are they used for? For example, would you build a modern office block in the middle of an historic village?

» How many roads service the building and how big are they? Is the road wide enough for all the sorts of vehicles that need to get to the building? Is there enough parking for the users of the building?

» How tall are the surrounding buildings? Will the new building throw a shadow on other areas? Will the building have enough natural light?

» What green space is there in the area and how is it used? For example, would you build a residential home for senior citizens next to an open space used regularly for sports?

» How will the building fit in with or enhance the surrounding landscape? For example, curved structures and the use of glass can make commercial buildings more attractive and less imposing: a tall glass building reflects the sky – a concrete one blocks the sky out.

» Will the local community use the building? Will the use of the building have any effect on the community? For example, a factory or warehouse may increase local traffic flow or create pollution. Will the building affect local property prices?

All these factors need to be taken into account when submitting plans to the local authority to get permission for any major construction project to go ahead.

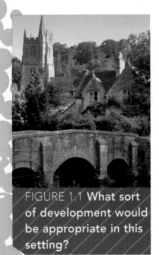

FIGURE 1.1 **What sort of development would be appropriate in this setting?**

Find out how legislation affects building design by interviewing architects, town planners, teachers or other experienced people. Try these questions.

✱ What could stop you from building a modern office block in the middle of an old, pretty village?

✱ What guidelines are there for designing road access and parking for different buildings?

Can you think of any other questions to ask?

When you have done your research, summarise your findings for this activity in a word-processed document.

LINKS

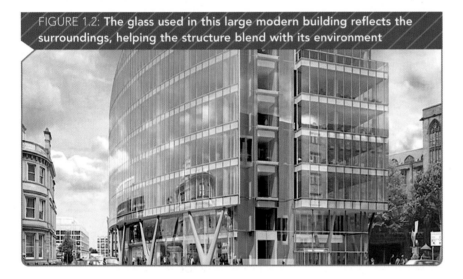

FIGURE 1.2: **The glass used in this large modern building reflects the surroundings, helping the structure blend with its environment**

Community consultations

The local community will be both disrupted by the actual building process and affected by the final design and use of any new building. It is important to make sure that the local community is well informed at every stage of a construction project and consulted about all the features of the design that may have an impact on their lives. If this is not done, and done well, community opposition can stop a project going ahead.

Depending on the size of the design project, community consultations may be:

» public meetings and exhibitions – held before the planning application is put in, giving the community the opportunity to comment on options for design proposals

» discussion groups (surgeries) – used to work out a solution where a particular community group may have an objection to a proposal

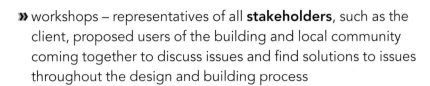

» workshops – representatives of all **stakeholders**, such as the client, proposed users of the building and local community coming together to discuss issues and find solutions to issues throughout the design and building process

» citizen panels – groups of local residents selected at random and asked to participate in research on specific design issues for a locality

» websites and media – used to keep the local community informed of design developments and to provide a focus for enquiries.

Enquiry by Design (EbD)

EbD is an initiative of the Prince's Foundation for the Built Environment. It is a way to make sure that everyone interested in the development of a site is consulted. The EbD involves developing a 'master plan' for the area detailing the local use of land and building styles. Technical workshops gather detailed information about the actual site and several stakeholder workshops develop a collective vision for the development.

Planning for Real®

This is a method of consulting the community developed by an organisation called The Neighbourhood Initiatives Foundation. The process involves contacting the community in and around a development area, building a model of the area with the community, looking at the development needs and options and drawing up a local action plan.

Working with a group of other learners, research the following websites and create a list of all the people that could be involved in consultations about the design for a site development. For each different group of people, try to think of their main concerns about the site.

✱ Birchfield Library, Birmingham – Community Consultation process:
http://www.birmingham.gov.uk/birchfieldconsultation.bcc

✱ The Glasshouse – community led design – Myatts Field Park project
http://theglasshouse.org.uk/gh_project.php?pr_id=11&pg_id=18&map=UK

✱ Enquiry by Design: http://www.princes-foundation.org/index.php?id=33

✱ Planning for real: http://www.nif.co.uk/planningforreal/

Factors affecting design

For each new building you need to research the location to find out what local factors might affect the design of the building, such as:

» How big is the space? Is the area flat? What sort of drainage does it have? Is it likely to subside or flood? What is the surrounding land like? What is it used for?

» How many people live locally? How does this affect the building?

» What is the existing infrastructure? Are there any roads to the site? Are there transport services, such as bus routes and railway stations? Does the site have water, gas or electricity supplies? Is the supply adequate?

Thinking about the purpose of the building and how it will be used will raise other factors affecting the design such as:

» Will the building be used by the local community? If so, what types of people, what are their needs and how often will they visit the building?

» Which designs fit different purposes, for example should the design for a courthouse or police station be different from the design for a theatre or an office block?

» The limits placed on the design by the amount of money available (budget) must also be considered.

» What will the budget allow?

» What is the cost of the land and the labour to build the structure?

» What funds are available for materials and which materials would be best for the type of building?

Social and economic effects

The construction industry provides the physical environment for human activities, such as houses, workplaces, schools, hospitals, cultural and leisure centres, shopping centres and the transport, communications, water, waste and power infrastructures that service these structures. The quality of the design can have a huge impact on the quality of life and health of the population. For example, early industrial towns had no open spaces, heavy pollution and closely packed houses. New designs are planned to have a positive effect on the health and well-being of the population, and to have no negative impact on the natural environment.

Good design can change the way people think about a place – a run down part of town can be regenerated into an area that attracts new business. This means that there are more jobs available, more money is earned by local workers and so the local economy thrives.

Design contributes to the economy throughout the lifespan of the building. Most buildings also have increased re-sale value due to the general rise in property prices over time. Well-designed buildings will increase in value at a higher rate than badly designed ones.

FIGURE 1.3 **Urban planning has come a long way since the industrial revolution**

MANAGE

Who pays for the design and construction of new buildings and structures?

Some buildings are **commissioned** and paid for by government departments or large businesses. Large residential developments may be funded by a **consortium** of property developers and builders. A new house may be paid for by the land owner and a **heritage** listed building may be renovated using funds from a charitable trust.

✱ Investigate the funding sources for five different building projects, either in your local area, or through research on the Internet.

✱ Describe the type of building project and identify the designer, the builder and the sources of funding for each project.

LINKS

Record the information from this activity in a table using word-processing or spreadsheet software.

✱ **Do designers, builders and funding organisations specialise in the types of buildings that they are involved with?**

✱ **Discuss your findings and the answer to the above question with your teacher and learner group.**

Pollution

Pollution is the introduction of unwanted or damaging elements into the environment. Pollution caused by buildings and their construction includes: noise, air, soil, water, visual and light pollution. The construction industry must make every effort to safeguard, maintain, improve and expand the built environment without harming the natural environment. It also has a duty to repair some of the damage done by the industry in the past. Look at 'Sustainability and environmental protection' later in this unit for more on this topic.

FIGURE 1.4 Appropriate disposal and recycling of waste is an important responsibility of the construction industry

Planning

Planning involves:

» working out how best to use different spaces

» making sure that the spaces are used effectively.

It is the responsibility of the local authority (council) to assess all plans for construction in their area. They can refuse to give planning permission or make permission dependent on changes to the plans. Local authorities also have a larger responsibility for the planning of infrastructure, public spaces and buildings, and the overall design and growth of their area.

The planning process

Designers and planners have to consider the way a building will fit with the plans for the area when they apply for planning permission to the local authority. The application for planning permission must include such information as:

» the design statement – a legal requirement for large projects under the Planning and Compulsory Purchase Act 2004

» drawings and models of the proposed structure

» evidence of consultations with the local community

» an Environmental Impact Assessment.

Each local authority has its own particular processes but most will involve:

» pre-application assistance – help with ensuring that the planning application contains all the necessary information

FIGURE 1.5 **Planning notices let local people know of plans for building work**

» consultation – inviting feedback on the plan by sending letters to people at neighbouring sites and putting notices near the site, at local public buildings and in the newspaper

» considering the design and consultation feedback – this may include a site visit; checking that the design complies with planning policies and legislation; and assessing the layout, appearance, materials to be used, access issues and the impact on the locality

» making a recommendation – the planning department will recommend to the Council that the planning application be approved or refused

» approval – the Councillors make the final decision. There is an appeal system if the plan is rejected.

THINK

Have a look at the design statement wizard for projects in the North East of England on the following website:

http://www.designstatement.co.uk/

You do not need to register to browse through the tool, only to save your design statement.

Click on each drop down menu to explore the number of options available under each section of the design statement. Do you understand all of the options listed? Discuss those that you do not understand with other learners and your teacher.

Now check the publications listed under the 'library icon' on this site. You will find some interesting material here, such as the **Environmental Impact Assessment** procedure.

http://www.designstatement.co.uk/library.php

Planning organisations

The Royal Town Planning Institute (RTPI) promotes good planning in the UK. Good planning should take into consideration space and place (spatial aspects); sustainability; integration with infrastructure, existing structures and use; the local environment; community opinions and future plans for the area.

An organisation called Urban Forum has produced 'The Handy Guide to Planning' which outlines the stages of the planning process in England and how community members can get involved.

RTPI
mediation of space · making of place

JOIN IN

What are the planning processes in your local area? How can you join in?

Visit the RTPI website and read 'The Handy Guide to Planning'.

http://www.rtpi.org.uk/

http://www.urbanforum.org.uk/pdf_files/plan_guide_final2-1.pdf

Find out what the planning processes are for your local area. If possible, get involved in some of the community consultation activities held by the local authority or other planning organisations.

Keep a journal of your 'joining in' activities and the outcomes of any meetings or consultations you attend.

After keeping notes on your involvement for a period of time (discuss the length of time with your teacher), put together a short report on your involvement with the planning process and present this to your learning group.

LINKS

A closer look at infrastructure

Infrastructure is the network of services to an area, such as roads, railway lines, airports, power lines, water and gas pipes, waste systems and telecommunications cables. A designer needs to assess the current infrastructure and find out what plans there are to change or improve infrastructure in the future, for example:

» new roads or road-widening projects

» upgrading water delivery and waste-water removal systems

» prospective sites for government or medical buildings, such as prisons and hospitals

» new or improved gas pipelines

» new railway lines and bridges.

Legislation

Legislation means any laws, regulations or other legal requirements that designers must take into account. For instance, there is legislation that applies to heritage protection, environmental issues and local needs. The following are examples of legislation you will need to know about.

» Town and country planning legislation – this is designed to preserve and enhance the environment and to help in resolving conflicts over the use of land, taking into account the needs of

FIND OUT

There is an Approved Code of Practice (ACoP) for the CDM regulations that gives practical advice for all those involved in construction work on how to comply with the law. Find out more about this at: http://www.hse.gov.uk/construction/cdm/acop.htm

the local community. There are three main Acts that you need to know about:

– the Town and Country Planning Act, 1990

– the Planning (Listed Buildings and Conservation Areas) Act, 1999

– the Planning (Hazardous Substances) Act, 1990.

» The Construction (Design Management) Regulations (CDM) 2007 – these regulations set out the health and safety duties of all parties involved in a construction project including the client, CDM co-ordinator, designers (anyone who prepares design drawings, specifications, bills of quantities and the specification of articles and substances), contractors and workers.

Stages of planning

There are several stages to any construction project, from demolishing existing buildings and clearing the site, to actual construction and use. You need good planning at every stage.

Demolition of existing structures

Methods of demolition include deconstruction, dismantling and mechanical site clearance. You need to consider the presence and removal of hazardous substances, such as asbestos, and prepare a very detailed health and safety plan. You also need to assess the effect of demolition on plants and animals on the site. Did you know, for instance, that you need special approval for the demolition of buildings and structures inhabited by bats!

FIGURE 1.6 Demolition can be particularly hazardous to the environment and must be undertaken with great care

Designing a sustainable built environment

Sustain means 'to keep going for a long time'. Building sustainability into construction projects involves thoughtful and careful planning, design and implementation of every aspect of the construction process.

Location

» Research the most suitable location for each construction.

» Assess the suitability of the structure to the landscape and environment or architectural period of surrounding buildings.

» Assess the affect the structure may have on the surroundings, including the local community and the effect on existing structures.

» Find out about existing infrastructure, amenities and transport.

Environmental impact

» Organise an Environmental Impact Assessment (EIA) on selected locations.

» Implement the recommendations.

An EIA is a full analysis of the potential environmental effects of a construction project. It should include the possible effects on water, air, noise, traffic and transport, landscape, urban design and wildlife.

Sustainable design principles

» Use of brownfield sites – this reduces the amount of building on rural sites. The government wants 60 per cent of new development to be on brownfield sites.

» Passive heating – the location and alignment of a building, placement of windows and careful selection of materials can make the best use of 'passive heat' – the warming effect of the sun – this will reduce energy consumption.

» Alternative energy technology – designing buildings with solar or **biomass** energy and heat pumps to reduce the amount of energy taken from the National Grid. As national energy is provided mainly by coal- or oil-fired power stations, which produce greenhouse gases, a reduction in the power they produce will also reduce greenhouse gases.

» Living roofs – these are roofs made of soil, turf and plants. They are good insulators (keeping heat inside the building and reducing energy consumption), improve air quality, reduce storm water run-off into rivers and provide habitats for birds.

» Use of locally sourced and sustainable materials – this reduces transport costs and pollution and supports the local economy. Sustainable materials are those made from renewable resources, using alternative energy sources – for example timber from a sustainable forestry plantation milled using wind power.

» Access – for buildings this includes ramps, lifts and stairs; for roads and railways it includes safe wildlife pathways underneath the structure.

» Open space – consider the basic human need for personal space. Good design should provide air, light, a sense of space and room for recreation.

» Make the structure long-lasting and low maintenance – these attributes will add to the energy-saving properties of the building.

» Meet the needs of the users – consider people's physical, mental and emotional health needs, for example security, recreation, accessibility, affordability, social interaction.

FIGURE 1.8 **Sustainable technology, such as this turf roof, helps reduce energy needs**

During construction and maintenance, you can improve sustainability by:

» using sustainable services, technologies and construction methods, including waste minimisation

» improving site and resource management – this includes working out ways to reduce waste of all types during a construction project, such as time, energy, resources and materials

» waste **reclamation** and recycling – involves sorting waste on-site into separate skips for **recycling**, for example paper, timber and brick, re-using materials wherever possible and using products made from recycled materials.

TEAMWORK

Investigate three of the following websites and prepare a short talk for your learning group.

a) Arup – Sustainable Project Appraisal Routine (SPeAR) http://www.arup.com/index.cfm

b) Building Research Establishment (BRE) – Environmental Assessment Method (BREEAM) http://www.breeam.org/

c) The Construction Industry Council Sustainable Development Committee www.cic.org.uk/activities/sustainComm.shtml

d) The national indicators for sustainable development http://www.sustainable-development.gov.uk/progress/national/index.htm

e) The Genesis Centre http://www.genesisproject.com/genesis05/

f) Green Construction http://www.nbsgreenconstruction.com/default.asp

Construction Industry Council

LINKS

Use word-processing or desktop publishing software to design a poster or brochure to help illustrate your talk.

The properties and uses of typical construction materials

A designer needs to think about the way materials behave, how strong they are, how they look and what they cost before choosing which materials to use in a design. The characteristics of the materials selected will dictate some elements of the design, for example a timber frame will support less load than a steel frame.

Properties of materials

You need to know what types of material are used in construction, how they are made, what their characteristics are and how they behave in different conditions.

The materials you use in construction have different characteristics, such as heaviness, strength, flexibility, fire resistance, elasticity, brittleness, combustibility, porosity or heat conduction. The characteristics of a material depend on its molecular content and structure and its mass, density and volume.

» Mass is the amount of matter (solid particles) in a compound; measured in kilograms (kg).

» Volume is the amount of space the material occupies; measured in cubic metres (m^3).

» Density is the amount of mass per unit volume of a material, measured in kilograms per cubic metre (kg/m^3).

Because different materials vary so much in structure and characteristics, they respond differently to forces or loads. A force or load may be the pressure (compression force) of the weight above the material, such as the weight of a multi-storey building pressing on its foundations; pulling or stretching forces, such as the tension on the cables of a suspension bridge; or pushing forces, such as strong wind.

Other commonly-used materials in construction:

Copper
Copper is a reddish metal. It can be easily bent and is used for gas and water pipes and for roofing and flashing.

Paint
New types of paint that contain no **petrochemicals** are now available – these reduce the impact on the environment and on the painter's health. The paints are either water-based or made using linseed or citrus oils. Pigments are organic – sourced from naturally occurring ores and plants.

More information about properties of materials can be found on the companion Teacher Resource Disk.

Plaster

Plaster is made from a calcium sulphate mineral known as gypsum. It is sold as a powder, then mixed with water to form a paste. It is quite soft when dry and can be sanded down, so it is used for finishing internal walls and ceilings – forming a smooth surface that can be painted, if required. It can also be moulded into ornate shapes such as ceiling roses. A mixture of plaster, sand, clay and straw is used for straw bale walls. Cement plaster can be used for fire-proofing.

Plastics

Produced as a by-product of the oil industry, plastics are very lightweight and do not absorb water, therefore they are not affected by frost.

There are two main types of plastic:

» thermoplastic – becomes soft when heated and hardens on cooling

» thermosetting – does not soften when heated but can char with excessive heat.

Plastics are used for: pipes, damp-proof courses, window frames, floor coverings, fillers and sealants, plugs, sockets, thermal insulators (plastic foam), light fittings and cable insulation, because they are good electrical insulators. Plastics are generally resistant to corrosion, except when used externally where some types can be degraded by ultraviolet (UV) light. Unplasticised polyvinyl-chloride (uPVC) is resistant to chemicals and can be used for underground pipes.

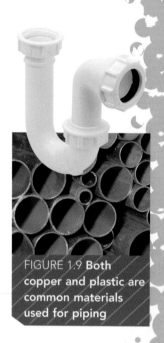

FIGURE 1.9 **Both copper and plastic are common materials used for piping**

Roof tiles

Roof tiles can be produced using clay, cement or slate. Solar tiles with built-in photo-voltaic cells are also available for use on south-facing roofs.

Sand

Sand is a naturally occurring substance made from broken down rocks, mostly quartz – silicon dioxide (SiO_2). Sand is used to make glass, concrete and bricks. It can also be used in paint to give a textured effect.

TRY THIS

Quarried rock, such as limestone, is used in a variety of different ways in construction. Have a look at the house on this website, which shows you how stone products are used:

http://www.tarmac.co.uk /quarryville/stoneSt/ house.html

TABLE 1.1 The properties of construction materials

Material	Density	Tensile strength	Compressive strength	Modulus of elas*
Bricks	varies. Generally around 1.85 g/cm³.	low.	ranges from 4 to 180 N/mm². Water content reduces compressive strength and thermal resistance.	very high.
Concrete	varies. Depends on the mix. High density concrete is about 2.5 g/cm³; low density concrete is 0.4 to 2.0 g/cm³.	very low. Only about 10 per cent of the compressive strength. Can be increased with reinforcement using steel.	varies. Depends on the type of aggregate used, air content and the free water to cement ratio. Reducing the free water to cement ratio increases the strength of concrete. If the mass of water in a concrete mixture is 40kg and the mass of cement is 80kg, the free water to cement ratio is 40/80 = 0.5.	high. Concrete is very stiff and brittle
Glass	varies. From less dense than aluminium to more dense than iron. Average 2.5 g/cm³.	low. Untreated glass is very brittle and breaks into sharp shards under tension.	high. Pure glass can withstand high compressive forces.	high.
Limestone	varies. Generally around 2.00 g/cm³.	low.	1,800–2,8000 psi.	high. Limestone is very stiff and brittle
Steel	high, 7.8 g/cm³.	high.	high. Steel can be subject to shearing forces under high compression loads. Shearing forces act parallel to the plane of the steel and cause a sliding failure.	high.
Timber	relatively low and varies depending on type. Usually between 0.5 and 0.7 g/cm³. The higher the density, the more strength the timber has.	high strength to mass ratio.	high strength to mass ratio. The dryer (more seasoned) the wood, the higher the strength. The strength of timber with a moisture content of 30 per cent is only about two-thirds the strength at 12 per cent moisture content.	

eat tolerance	Corrosion resistance	
ery high.	medium. Bricks can be subject to frost and salt damage.	Bricks are hard-wearing, low-maintenance and attractive building materials made from clay, sometimes with other chemicals added during manufacture. The clay is pressed into moulds and fired at temperatures up to 1000°C. Most bricks are rectangular; the most common size is 215 x 102 x 65mm.
gh.	relatively low. Concrete contains calcium carbonate, which is soluble in acids, such as rainwater. It also reacts with iron oxide (rust).	Concrete is a low-cost material manufactured using: » 7 to 15 per cent cement » 60 to 80 per cent aggregate (sand, gravel, crushed rock) » 14 to 21 per cent water. The properties of concrete depend on the type and amount of cement and aggregate and on the water to cement ratio. Concrete has many uses in construction from foundations to major structural use when it is reinforced with steel bars and mesh. Concrete is liable to corrosion and this should be taken into account when deciding on materials to use.
gh. Glass has a very gh melting point.	very high.	Glass is made from quartz sand, which is almost 100 per cent crystalline silica (silicon dioxide, SiO_2). Most types of glass contain about 70 per cent silica. Soda-lime glass contains almost 30 per cent sodium and calcium oxides or carbonates. Glass is used for glazing windows and doors; glass fibre is used in optical cables, to reinforce plastic products and in thermal insulation. The properties of glass can be modified with the addition of other compounds or heat treatment.
gh.	relatively low. Limestone is made of calcium or magnesium carbonate, which is soluble in acids, such as rainwater.	Limestone is an ornamental grey or yellow stone made from calcium carbonate and quarried all over the UK. It is strong and easily cut into blocks. It is often used for building external walls – for example the Houses of Parliament and St Paul's Cathedral are built from different types of limestone. Polished limestone can be used internally as a decorative stone. Crushed limestone is used as an **aggregate** in concrete.
gh. Carbon steel gins to lose ength at mperatures above 0°C and reduces in ength at a steady te up to 800°C.	medium to high. Stainless steel containing nickel and chromium is highly resistant to corrosion and fire.	Steel is an expensive but hard-wearing material made from iron with between 0.2 and 1.7 per cent carbon. High carbon content makes steel harder but more brittle. Other additions may include: » nickel and manganese – to increase tensile strength » chromium – to increase hardness and melting point » vanadium – to increase hardness and resistance to fatigue. Standards used for steel are: » 2005 AISC Specification for Structural Steel Buildings » 2004 RCSC Specification for Structural Joints Using ASTM A325 or A490 Bolts » 2005 AISC Code of Standard Practice for Steel Buildings and Bridges.
v compared to er construction terials. But thick ber has relatively od structural egrity in fire.	low. Timber has low resistance to damp, fungal and insect attack. Wet and dry rot causes decay and loss of strength.	Timber is a renewable construction material used for framework, joists, studs, floorboards and doors. There are two types of timber: » softwood – from coniferous trees, such as pine » hardwood – from deciduous trees, such as ash and oak. The characteristics of timber vary greatly.

How materials affect design

During the design process the choice of materials is determined by:

» functional demands

» Building Regulations

» availability

» cost.

Modern Methods of Construction (MMC) favour materials that contribute to the efficiency of the construction process. For example, using composite products such as pre-assembled concrete panels reduces on-site labour requirements, wastage and errors. This results in:

» higher health and safety standards on-site

» greater compliance with sustainable ethics

» superior finishes to products.

Think about the materials that you have used.

» What construction materials or products do you use that are processed or manufactured in your local area?

» Are the materials produced using sustainability principles?

» What do you use the materials for?

Tabard Square is a development of 517 residential apartments set around a landscaped public square in the London Borough of Southwark. The development was overall winner of the Housing Design Awards in 2007.

I want to be...

...an architect

» What particular skills do you need to be an architect and what made you choose this job?

You need to have good attention to detail, be able to think laterally and to consider how others will use or perceive a space or building. Architecture has always interested me because it is all around us – bad or good, it forms the environment in which we all live.

» Which buildings do you find inspiring and could you explain why?

There are many examples, but the Lloyds building in London is a good example, as it provides a new concept of inside-out and visual transparency. I like buildings that are constructed from high-quality materials that still look as fresh tens of years after construction.

» How do you make sure that a design fits in with the local landscape or surrounding buildings?

You can use sympathetic materials and massing. Also you can pick up on certain design keys, such as the proportion of windows etc, without needing to mimic period details in inferior form.

» What materials do you select for your designs and why?

Economic considerations often have a bearing on those elements that are not seen – e.g. steel frame versus concrete frame – and some traditional construction methods have greater design restrictions – the size of windows, for example.

» How do you make sure you consider the opinions of the community or the users of a structure? What sort of input do you get from these consultations

Consultation with the community is often used on larger schemes, and highlights concerns of local neighbours, which can often be addressed at initial design stage. Any project with a specific user will involve extensive discussions to ensure that we, as designers, understand their needs, and that the building functions in a way that suits their business activity, and from an aesthetic point of view represents the company's image or aspirations.

» What is the hardest part of your job?

Bridging the gap between client aspirations and budget.

» What is the best part of your job as an architect?

I enjoy solving problems, and adding value by design.

Steve Jones

Site Visit

Tabard Square →

The judges used these criteria, among others, to choose the winning design:

» Is it a good streetscape?

» Will people want to live here?

» Are all the details right?

» How will initial appeal be sustained for future generations?

Tabard Square has three low-rise apartment blocks, a 22-storey tower, a crèche, a supermarket and a large open space with a sports pavilion and restaurant. The tower has balconies on all the apartments and a roof garden. The square is open to the public during the day but closes using special moving sculptures at night.

In the annual essay on the state of house-building 2007, Melanie Howard writes, that residential projects need to have:

» more relaxed and informal meeting spaces

» more flexible use of space in homes

» access to safe green space

» sustainability features.

Find out more about Tabard Square at http://www.designforhomes.org/hda/2007/complete/tabard.html and decide whether you think it covers all of Melanie's points.

**Tabard Square –
who did what?**

Architect Rolfe
Judd

Developer Berkeley
Homes? East
Thames

Contractor Laing
O'Rourke

Planning Authority
London Borough of
Southwark

Give your own design award

Find a building that you think is really well-designed and
attractive – it could be a home you would like to live in, a
public building, office or an industrial building. Look in your
local area, or in architectural and construction magazines or on
websites.

List the reasons why you would give your chosen building an
award including:

» how the building fits in with the characteristics of the locality

» what sustainability features the building has

» how the building will be used

» what features of the design make the building attractive and fit for
the purpose.

Assessment Tips

To pass your assessment for this unit you need to consider very carefully all the project information that you will be given by your teacher. This should include:

» a description of the proposals for a small construction project

» drawings including: plans; elevations; a site layout drawing, showing the positions of the mains, utilities and the required service entry points.

 — E-portfolio —

Create a Word file for your notes and insert a header and footer. Put your name, candidate number, centre name and centre number in the header and use the page numbering feature in the footer. Sketches should be no larger than A3 and should be included in your portfolio.

You need to prepare planning advice for each stage of the design process, giving reasons for the different stages.

Have you included:

The human and physical factors that will influence the design process and final design, and the impacts of these. ☐

The major stages of the planning process and the purposes of all of these. ☐

The sustainability and environmental protection influences on the design of the project. ☐

The reasons for the use of specific materials. ☐

FIND OUT

» What is the land surrounding the site used for? How does the building fit in with or enhance the landscape?

» Is the project site surrounded by buildings? How old are these? What is the style? What are they used for? How tall are they? Will the new project throw a shadow on other areas?

» What is the existing infrastructure? How many roads service the project site? How wide are they? Is there enough parking for the users of the building? Are there utility services already in place? Do these have enough capacity for the project?

» Will the local community use the building – or will the use of the building have an effect on the community? Will the building affect local property prices?

» Should there be an Environmental Impact Assessment? Will the project use sustainable services, technologies and construction methods, including waste minimisation? Are there plans to reduce waste of all types during the construction project, including wasted time, energy, resources and materials?

» Which materials will be used and why are these the most suitable?

» When you have gathered the relevant information – prepare your advice as a planning consultant to the project

SUMMARY / SKILLS CHECK

» The influence of human and physical factors on design – These factors include:
- ✓ the characteristics of the locality and surrounds, including the existing infrastructure
- ✓ community consultations and the use of processes such as Enquiry by Design (EbD) and Planning for Real ®
- ✓ factors affecting design, including the social and economic effects of constructions and pollution.

» Planning – Issues covered include:
- ✓ infrastructure needs
- ✓ the local authority planning process – pre-application, consultation, feedback, recommendation, approval or appeal
- ✓ legislation, including town and country planning legislation, Construction (Design Management) Regulations (CDM) 2007 and the Approved Code of Practice (ACoP) for the CDM regulations
- ✓ stages of planning, including demolition, design, building and maintenance
- ✓ Planning Policy Guidance (PPG) and Statements (PPS).

» Sustainability – Sustainability and environmental protection issues include:
- ✓ why we need to respect the natural environment
- ✓ how to reduce waste and pollution, control consumption, conserve natural assets and preserve wildlife, flora and fauna
- ✓ designing a sustainable built environment
- ✓ Environmental Impact Assessments (EIA)
- ✓ sustainable design principles, such as the use of brownfield sites, passive heating, alternative energy technology, locally sourced and sustainable materials.

» Materials – This unit has covered:
- ✓ the properties and uses of common construction materials such as bricks, concrete, copper, glass, limestone, paint, plaster, plastics, roof tiles, sand, steel and timber
- ✓ the ways that the properties of these materials affect and influence design.

OVERVIEW

A construction designer can be an architect, a civil or structural engineer, or a design technician. The first things a construction designer must consider are the conditions of the proposed building's location. These include the **topography**, ground conditions and movement, and weather conditions. In the UK there is a shortage of land for building, especially in inner-city areas. Design solutions need to make the best use of the available area while keeping a sense of space both inside and around the building. The design must be suitable for the function of the building (such as living space, commercial, community, etc.) and be '**buildable**' – that is using materials and construction skills that are readily available in the local area.

At the start of a project the designer and design team receive a brief from their client. They then use their creative skills, together with an understanding of **structural forms** and construction materials, to produce scale drawings and models of possible design solutions to present to the client and to the general public. The designer must be able to explain the choices of structural form, design, materials and **components** to the client – and how these choices fit the design brief. The client may propose modifications to the design solution. The designer must therefore have the communication and negotiation skills to discuss design options and agree on a final approach. Detailed design drawings and specifications must then be prepared for the construction team to work from.

During construction, project teams plan the sequence of the work to be done, communicate openly and work co-operatively to ensure that the project is a success. The designer and the design team assist with interpretation of the drawings and specifications, ensuring that the work proceeds according to the design specifications and in making any alterations or adjustments that may be required.

The work of a design technician is very varied – from the creative aspects of producing design solutions to the nuts and bolts on-site work.

Aesthetics

Aesthetic means pleasing to the eye. The aesthetic appeal of a design is affected by its proportions, **unity**, **balance** and **symmetry**.

The proportions of a building include:

» the size of the building in relation to the size of the whole site

» the overall size and shape of rooms – this will vary for different purposes

» the relationship between the length, width and height of a room – a room that is long and thin would be the wrong proportions for a living area, but the right proportions for a hallway

» the number and size of openings, such as doors and windows.

Unity is about having something in common, for example:

» the various parts of a building looking as though they belong together – there may be a certain shape or feature repeated across the structure

» a building or structure looking as though it belongs in the area – it fits in with the other structures around it, or complements the landscape.

Balance and symmetry – a building should have a focal point – this is usually the entrance. The size and shape of the building should be balanced around this point. The building may be completely symmetrical, or have a balanced but asymmetrical shape.

FIGURE 2.3 **Symmetrical and asymmetrical structures: the Natural History Museum in London, and the Guggenheim Museum, Bilbao, both display balance**

Structural forms

The two main structural forms are:

» **rectilinear** – for example using beams, posts and lintels; cross-walls or frames to form rectangular shapes

» **curvilinear** – for example using domes, arches or geodesic domes to form curved shapes.

For low-rise buildings, the main structural forms are:

» **masswall** structural form – solid walls define the space inside the building and support the load; masswalls may be:

– monolithic – using cast concrete floors and walls, for example in blocks of flats

– cellular – using bonded brickwork for both external and internal walls, each of which may be load bearing, for example houses

– crosswall – parallel walls carry loading and internal space is divided using non load-bearing block or timber-stud partition walls, for example in terraced houses

» **framed structures** – using steel or reinforced concrete frames to carry the load – internal walls may be load bearing to support the structure of the frame

– timber frame – used for external and internal walls of buildings no higher than three storeys. Cladding on the frame may chosen to improve rigidity, for example in small offices

– skeletal structure – rectangular frame made using steel, reinforced concrete, and in some cases laminated timber, for example offices, shops, hotels

– portal frames – using a steel or concrete frame with spanning or supporting members to form structures with no internal columns, for example warehouses and large factories

– shed structures – similar to portal frames but with the span between supporting members filled with braced girders or roof trusses

– shell – some structures have a curved membrane surface – the shell structure can be much thinner than masonry. The Millennium Dome – now the O_2 is an example of this.

» whether the design will look dated or out of place in the future – if so, will this matter?

» the buildability of the design – how easy will it be to construct? For example consider these questions:

- What skills will be required to build the design?

- Are these skills available locally or will specialists have to be brought in?

- What materials will be used?

- Are these supplied locally – or will they have to be transported?

- Will the cost of materials be within budget?

- Does the design allow for **constraints** – are these included in the timeframe?

MANAGE

1. Research the design brief, plans and specifications for a two-storey building.

   You could do either of the following:

   ✱ Download and examine the England and Wales Cricket Board (ECB) Guidance notes on designing a cricket pavilion or clubhouse from the ECB website: http://static.ecb.co.uk/files/ts5-pavilions-and-clubhouses-1336.pdf

   ✱ Obtain a design brief, plans and specifications from your tutor.

   Consider each item listed on the design brief and check the plans and specifications to find out how the requirements have been incorporated into the design.

2. Create a design solution for a youth club/Internet café

   Design brief: accessible location, adequate accommodation, contemporary appearance, bright decoration, robust fixtures and fittings, cutting-edge technologies.

   Prepare a scale drawing for the project and identify the component parts, materials and skills required to build the design.

Prepare a short talk, using the design brief, plans and specifications, to demonstrate how elements of the brief have been incorporated into the design of the project.

Keep the project documentation and the notes for your talk in your evidence portfolio.

L I N K S

Present and discuss your design with the client

When you have prepared the drawings or models for the selected design solution and the specifications of materials and components, you need to prepare for meeting the client. You should be confident and enthusiastic about your design, but prepared to take on board any suggestions that the client may have.

The client will be very keen to check that the proposed design fits the design brief in every way. You should double-check that you have included all the points in the brief. The client's taste and preferences may be different from yours, but one is not more correct than the other. Remember, the client is the one paying for the project so you need to listen carefully to ideas and suggestions and be diplomatic when debating and negotiating changes. In some cases it may not be possible to comply with all of the client's ideas or elements of the design brief.

There may be planning restrictions, environmental or other regulations, issues with the landscape or ground conditions, or issues with the availability of requested materials or skills. If there are some elements of the design brief that have been excluded – for a good reason – make sure that you point these out and explain them straight away. Don't wait for the client to find out and question these points. Put your argument clearly and tactfully and provide any evidence, such as planning regulations.

Careers in design and construction

The construction industry offers a wide choice of careers and career pathways in design.

The design team

A design team may consist of:

» architects, who generally lead the design team and liaise with the client

» architectural technicians, architectural technologists or building engineers, who provide technical and advisory support

FIND OUT

Find out more about PRP at http://www.prparchitects.co.uk/practice/

FIGURE 2.9 **Grange Primary School – one of PRP's architectural projects**

Questions

» Would you prefer to work for a large or small company?

» What are the advantages of working for a large company like PRP?

» Would you like to work locally or have the opportunity to travel?

» Find out what international projects PRP have been involved in.

» Look at some of the new projects that PRP have designed – do you notice any themes or common features? Which ones do you like the most?

Assessment Tips

Building on the work that you have done throughout this unit, you can:

– prepare a checklist of the points you will need to consider before sketching a design solution

– list the types of sketches and drawings that you would prepare, including the scale to be used, and the features that should be included in each one.

Your role as a design technician

Task One: Prepare sketches and a 3D model for a two-storey building

To pass your assessment for this unit you need to consider very carefully all the project information that you will be given by your teacher. This should include: a design brief for a proposed simple two-storey construction project; a site layout for the project.

Task Two: Role play

Make notes for the role play, including:

» the job role and responsibilities of a design technician

» your role within the design team

» your qualifications and your development or career path

» the names and roles of relevant professional bodies

» factors to include when describing to a client how a design meets their needs.

E-portfolio

Create a Word file for your notes and insert a header and footer. Put your name, candidate number, centre name and centre number in the header and use the page numbering feature in the footer. Sketches should be no larger than A3 and should be included in your portfolio.

For your 3D model, consider and keep notes on:

– the scale you will use for the model

– materials you will use, such as wood, plastic, metal and cardboard

– finishing to be applied, such as spray or hand painting

– design features to be included in the model such as trees and garden areas

– photographs to be taken at different stages and of the completed model.

Have you included:

A design for a simple building or structure and reasons for your design choices.

Simple sketches and photographs of a scale model for a simple structure and notes on how you will describe the design to a client. ☐

A list of the major job roles in construction and the training options for these.

A report on teamwork in the construction industry. ☐ ☐

SUMMARY / SKILLS CHECK

» Construction designers

✓ Construction designers work from a detailed design brief to develop creative ideas for a structure. They need excellent drawing skills and they must be creative and imaginative – but they also need to be methodical, careful and precise when producing detailed drawings. Design drawings include sketches, plans, elevations, perspectives, detailed design and working drawings.

» Design choices

✓ When making design choices you need to consider: what land is available, what the site conditions are like, the population density, the aesthetics of the design and the structural form for the building – this could be:

- rectilinear – for example using beams, posts and lintels; crosswalls or frames to form rectangular shapes

- curvilinear – for example using domes, arches or geodesic domes to form curved shapes.

» Working to a brief

✓ A design brief is a document that outlines the basic requirements of the structure to be built. When considering a design solution you need to think about: how long the structure is expected to last, how the building will be used – now and in the future – and the buildability of the design, that is, how easy it will be to construct.

» Construction teams

✓ A design team may consist of: architects, architectural technicians, architectural technologists or building engineers, structural engineers, quantity surveyors, service engineers.

✓ A construction project team includes:

- professional and technologist personnel – those that generally require a degree or similar level of qualification, such as architects, construction technologists, engineers, surveyors and managers

- craftspeople – skilled trades that require some level of qualification, such as bricklaying, carpentry and joinery, plumbing, painting and decorating and electrical installation

- operatives – semi or unskilled jobs that often don't require any qualification, such as scaffolding and labouring.

OVERVIEW

This unit introduces you to the tools and activities associated with construction trades including: bricklaying, carpentry and joinery, painting and decorating, electrical trades, plumbing.

People skilled in these trades are always in demand and the expected standard of work is very high. All successful tradespeople have a strong focus on two main factors: quality, and health and safety. These two factors depend on the ability to select the correct tools, materials and equipment for the job and to use them properly, following the recommended safe work methods.

Both you and your employer have responsibilities under occupational health and safety **legislation**. Your main responsibility is to follow all the recommended health and safety procedures in the workplace. In addition to the safe use of tools, you need to know the correct procedures for working in hazardous conditions, such as at heights or in confined spaces. It is also important to avoid accidents and injury by using correct methods for lifting and moving heavy items.

Each of the crafts covered in this chapter use a particular set of tools – you must understand how to care for your tools and use them correctly. You need to know the safety issues associated with each one, for example, some tools are sharp and you could injure yourself quite seriously if you don't use them properly.

Finally, when you are working in your chosen craft area, you will need to be able to understand and interpret written information and drawings which specify what and how work has to be done and what materials should be used. The construction industry uses standard signs, symbols and notations for drawings and documents to make sure everyone using the documents has the same understanding of what they mean.

and include:

» type of cable containment system, such as steel conduit

» cable type, size (outside diameter) and fixing method

» material choice for fittings and fixtures, such as switches and plug sockets, for example plastic or metal.

Specifications for plumbing work
These include details of the type and size of valves, pipes, fittings and connectors, for example copper or plastic. Specific information about appliances, for instance boilers, and fittings such as washbasins and bathtubs, are given, including the model number.

CHECK IT OUT

View the detailed material specifications for kit log homes at the following website:

http://www.logcabinhome. co.uk/garden-summer-houses/log-homes-garden-houses-specification.html

Identify materials and components for your work

A tradesperson needs to understand how to translate design documents into a real product. You need to be able to interpret:

» sketches

» symbols

» drawings

» notes

» scales

» abbreviations.

There are standard conventions used in the construction industry, to make sure that everyone interprets these things correctly.

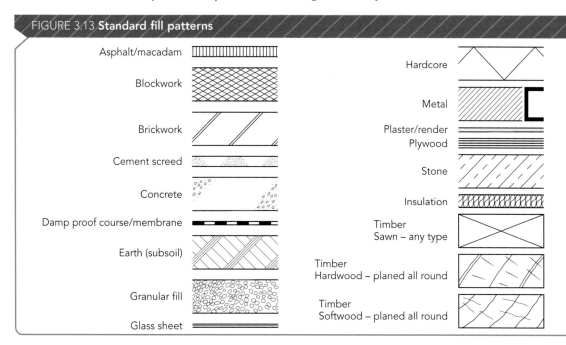

FIGURE 3.13 **Standard fill patterns**

Asphalt/macadam
Blockwork
Brickwork
Cement screed
Concrete
Damp proof course/membrane
Earth (subsoil)
Granular fill
Glass sheet

Hardcore
Metal
Plaster/render
Plywood
Stone
Insulation
Timber Sawn – any type
Timber Hardwood – planed all round
Timber Softwood – planed all round

You need to know the standard conventions used for specifying materials on drawings and have an up-to-date working knowledge of new products and their applications. A competent tradesperson can read a drawing and:

» identify all the materials required

» identify potential problems

» estimate labour hours for completion.

Manufacturers' data sheets may provide extra information not readily apparent from the design team's specifications, for example the drying times of products such as paints: you need this information to plan your work and assess how long it will take – this is the level of productivity.

Use a range of hand tools

The efficiency and quality of your work depends on your skills and experience and your ability to:

» clean, maintain and store your tools to keep them in the best working order

» select the correct tools and equipment for each different part of a job, including PPE

» accurately measure, mark and set out your work

» use the selected tools safely and correctly

» keep the work area tidy and secure

» reduce waste and dispose of any waste correctly.

Bricklayer

A bricklayer uses masonry products such as stone, bricks and blocks, and mortar mixtures to build new internal and external walls and to carry out restoration and maintenance work to existing buildings.

CHECK IT OUT

Visit the DIY Data website for some tips on how to build a brick wall:

http://www.diydata.com/techniques/brickwork/wall/brick_wall.php

A bricklayer uses the following hand tools:

- brick trowel
- pointing trowel
- spirit level
- string, lines, pins and corner blocks
- guage lathe
- steel tape measure

- brick marking guage
- builder's square
- sliding bevel
- club hammer
- brick hammer
- bolster chisel

- plugging chisel
- cold chisel
- jointing iron
- jointing raker or chariot
- soft hand brush.

More information about bricklaying tools can be found on the companion Teacher Resource Disk.

Tool-care tips

- Take care of tools by keeping them in a toolbag or toolbox.

- Clean and dry tools carefully after use, some may require a light coat of oil to prevent rusting.

- store tools safely, for example in a security hut, tool vault, site van or lockable cabin. Keep cutting edges sharp and clean.

Carpenter and joiner

A joiner usually works in the workshop making items such as doors, door frames, windows and kitchen units. A carpenter usually works on-site fitting, fixing and installing timber doors, windows, floors, roofs, stairs and partitions.

A carpenter uses the following hand tools:

- hand saws
- chisels
- hammers
- screwdrivers

- planes, files and rasps
- hand-boring tools
- measuring and marking tools
- clamps.

Painter and decorator

A painter and decorator uses a variety of hand tools for preparing internal or external walls or decorative fixtures, such as ceiling roses and applying paint or wallpaper.

A painter and decorator uses the following hand tools:

CHECK IT OUT

Visit the DIY Data website for some tips on how to make a garden gate:

http://www.diydata.com/projects/build_gate/garden_gates.php

More information about carpentry and joinery tools can be found on the companion Teacher Resource Disk.

More information about painting and decorating tools can be found on the companion Teacher Resource Disk.

CHECK IT OUT

Visit the DIY Data website for some tips on how to prepare a wall for painting:

http://www.diydata.com/decorating/painting_walls/paint_preparation.php

» paint scraper

» filling knife

» putty knife

» shave hook

» paint rollers

» paint brushes

» hand board

» paint kettles and roller trays

» paste board

» paste bucket

» wallpapering brushes

» knives, scissors and shears

» rules

» plumb bob.

Electricians

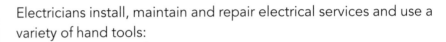

Electricians install, maintain and repair electrical services and use a variety of hand tools:

» pliers

» wire cutters

» wire strippers

» screwdrivers

» hammers

» knives

» hacksaws

» files and rasps.

More information about electrician's tools can be found on the companion Teacher Resource Disk.

Plumbers

Plumbers install, maintain and repair water, and gas services and roofs.

Plumbers use a variety of hand tools including:

» pliers

» snips

» hammers

» knives

» saws

» pipe-cutters

» grips and wrenches

» spanners

» sheet metal formers

» abraders, rasps and files

» pipe benders

» pressure testers

» blow torch.

CHECK IT OUT

Visit the DIY Data website for some tips on working with copper pipe

http://www.diydata.com/materials/copper_pipe/copper_pipe.php

More information about plumber's tools can be found on the companion Teacher Resource Disk.

Personal protective equipment is used when the safest work method for a task still involves some risk of injury. You need to know how to keep PPE in good condition – inspect equipment regularly for cracks, dents or tears and report faulty equipment to your supervisor for replacement.

Hazardous substances on construction sites include: concrete, dust, paints, solvents, mastics, adhesives, fungicide, fuel, chemicals, asbestos and lead. The Control of Substances Hazardous to Health Regulations 2002 (COSHH) covers safe handling of hazardous substances except asbestos and lead. Specific laws apply to these two substances.

» Safe working practices

✔ Some basic safe working practices you should understand and follow are:

- good housekeeping
- safe manual handling
- safe work in confined spaces
- safe work below ground level
- safe work at heights.

» Drawings and specifications

✔ Craftspeople work from drawings and specifications, which show the measurements and materials to be used for each job. A tradesperson needs to understand how to translate design documents into a real product. You need to be able to interpret sketches, drawings, scales, symbols, notes and abbreviations.

» Hand tools and working practices

✔ Craftspeople use a range of hand tools. The efficiency and quality of your work depends on your skills and experience and your ability to:

- keep your tools in good condition
- select the correct tools and use them safely
- make accurate measurements
- keep your work area tidy and secure
- reduce waste and dispose of any waste correctly.

OVERVIEW

Construction methods have evolved over time, using new materials and technology to improve the safety and efficiency of construction activities and the sustainability of structures. You need to know what materials and methods are available now, and to keep yourself informed of new methods and materials as they are developed and introduced. Keeping up to date is very important. Changes in the industry are rapid – responding to the need for more effective and sustainable materials and processes.

The construction industry offers a wide range of careers in areas such as planning and design, new build, restoration and renovation, and maintenance and repair. Within these areas there are different types of job and skill levels. Each job requires a unique set of skills and training. You need to consider which types of work match your own abilities and preferences. Professional positions such as engineers and managers normally require a degree or similar level of qualification. Craft jobs include the skilled trades, such as bricklaying, carpentry and joinery, plumbing, painting and decorating, and electrical installation.

Other jobs in the industry are at the operative level – that is not fully qualified, although a skilled operative may have some training and several years of experience. An unskilled operative could be just starting training, or working as a general labourer.

You can progress from a general operative to craftsperson, manager, architect or engineer – your choice!

Create the Built Environment: Methods & Materials

04

Skills list

At the end of this unit, you should:

» know about modern construction methods, materials and techniques

» understand the use of sustainable materials

» understand the job roles, career opportunities and progression routes, and the importance of teamwork, for those who construct the built environment.

Job watch

Examples of jobs involved in construction from planning and design to building and maintenance include:

» engineer
» construction technologist
» architect
» surveyor
» manager
» bricklayer
» carpenter and joiner
» plumber
» painter and decorator
» electrician
» skilled operative
» unskilled operative.

Modern construction methods materials and techniques

The construction industry is constantly looking for ways to improve the quality and sustainability of the built environment, and the safety, efficiency and environmental friendliness of materials and methods. Areas of improvement include:

» use of machinery (plant)

» modern construction techniques

» new materials.

FIGURE 4.1 **Use of plant, such as these cranes and hoists, makes new and ambitious construction techniques possible**

Plant used in the construction industry

Machinery and equipment used in the construction industry is called plant. It is designed to reduce the time and manual effort required to do a job, make more ambitious methods possible and improve safety. There are both environmental and health and safety issues related to using machinery – for example noise and air pollution, and hand-arm vibration syndrome.

Construction companies hire most of their plant from hire companies as and when they need it. This reduces capital costs – they don't have to buy expensive equipment outright – and the costs of maintenance and storage between jobs. Orders for plant

Who works in the construction industry?

There are more than two million people working in and for the construction industry in the UK. We have looked at the jobs of construction professionals, designers and some skilled crafts and trades in previous units. Here we shall examine how you train for some of these jobs and how they, and other job roles, co-operate in a construction team.

Job roles in construction

Construction jobs tend to fall into the following broad categories:

» operative – unskilled and partly skilled labourers

» craft and trade – traditional trades and craftspeople such as bricklayers and carpenters and including building services engineers, such as plumbers

» technical – surveyors, engineers, architectural technicians

» administrative and supervisory – estimators, quality surveyors, building surveyors, clerks of works

» professional – architects, designers

» managerial – project managers.

There is often a functional overlap between these jobs. Teamwork is vital in construction – people in all these different job roles need to discuss the design, specifications, workflow and interaction of different stages of the work with each other and co-operate to make sure that the project is a success.

Craftspeople and building service engineers

Craft jobs include: trowel occupations, carpentry and joinery, plastering, roofing, tiling, and painting and decorating.

People in building services job roles make buildings comfortable, energy-efficient and safe. Heating, ventilation, air-conditioning, lighting, power, telecommunications, plumbing, drainage, fire protection and even the installation of noise management material are completed by workers in the building service engineering area.

Most people in crafts and building services start with an apprenticeship. These are available in construction (craft), electrical and electronic servicing, mechanical engineering services and plumbing. An apprenticeship is half training course, half work. You apply for an apprenticeship just like any other job. You can start any time from your 16th birthday up to your 25th birthday. Depending on the workplace, the training required, the training providers available and the type of apprenticeship, your apprenticeship could take between one and five years to complete. A fully-qualified craftsperson may work alone, or supervise one or more general operatives, and on large projects may work under the direction of a technician or professional manager. Apprenticeships in buildings services include: plumbing, heating, ventilating, air-conditioning and refrigeration (HVACR) and electrotechnical. Most building services engineers are self-employed in owner-operated businesses.

Engineering construction technicians

Engineering construction technicians work for engineers and may supervise a team of craftspeople or building service engineers. Their work involves planning, designing and creating pipe and ductwork systems or building frameworks. Training for this occupation includes:

» National Apprenticeship Scheme for Engineering Construction (NASEC)

» BTEC Certificate/Diploma in Operations and Maintenance Engineering

» BTEC Certificate/Diploma in Mechanical or Electrical Engineering

» City & Guilds Progression Award in Applying Engineering Principles (6983) Levels 1 and 2

» City & Guilds Certificate in Engineering (2800) Level 3

» Foundation degree or BTEC HNC/HND in Engineering.

Building surveyors

Building surveyors understand the legislation, regulations, standards and codes of practice relevant to construction. They supervise projects for the local council, conservation organisations or large construction firms, making sure everything is done

CHECK IT OUT

Find out more about becoming an engineering construction technician on the Learn Direct website:

http://www.learndirect-advice.co.uk/helpwithyour career/jobprofiles/profiles/profile939/

correctly. Building surveyors also give advice to builders, owners and facility managers on details for the design, construction, maintenance, repair, renovation and conservation of all types of building.

Most building surveyors have a degree in surveying, construction, civil engineering or building engineering. Some people begin with a BTEC HNC/HND or foundation degree in surveying or construction, start work as a surveying technician and study further while working.

Civil or structural engineers

Civil engineers plan, manage, design and supervise construction or maintenance projects on fixed structures such as bridges, power plants, roads, railways, dams and flood management structures. Structural engineering is one area of civil engineering concerned with ensuring that constructions can withstand all the weight, stresses and pressures exerted on the structure. Stresses include natural elements, such as wind and seismic forces.

To become a structural engineer you need to complete a three-year Bachelor of Engineering (BEng) degree or a four-year Master's (MEng) degree in structural engineering or civil engineering. Alternatively, you can start at the technician level by completing a BTEC HNC/HND or foundation degree in engineering, then continuing training on the job.

Estimators or cost engineers

Estimators work out how much a construction project will cost. They need to research information about the staff and skills, materials and equipment required for each job and get quotes from suppliers and sub-contractors. Estimators usually progress into the job from administrative, craftsperson, technician or surveying assistant work, or by doing an engineering apprenticeship or studying for a BTEC HNC/HND or degree in civil engineering or construction.

Qualifications that you could gain while working as an estimator include:

» NVQ in Project Control Levels 3 and 4

» NVQ in Construction Contracting Operations Levels 3 and 4

» Certificate and Diploma in Site Management Level 4.

CHECK IT OUT

Find out more about becoming a building surveyor on the Learn Direct website:

http://www.learndirect-advice.co.uk/helpwithyour career/jobprofiles/profiles/ profile481

CHECK IT OUT

Find out more about becoming a structural engineer on the Learn Direct website:

http://www.learndirect-advice.co.uk/helpwithyour career/jobprofiles/profiles/ profile1445/

CHECK IT OUT

Find out more about becoming an estimator, or cost engineer, on the Learn Direct website:

http://www.learndirect-advice.co.uk/helpwithyour career/jobprofiles/profiles/ profile834/

Teamwork

Each team member will bring a specific set of skills and expertise to the project, but in addition to this, all construction team members must have:

» a complete and correct understanding of the goals and timelines of the project

» a commitment to the specified quality standards and the values of the client, for example to sustainable construction practices

» a commitment to open and honest communication, particularly regarding mistakes, breakdowns and other problems that may affect the project

» trust in, and respect for, the client and other members of the team.

Each of the team members will have particular roles and responsibilities involving interaction with other members of the team. It is important that communication about project progress is:

» regular and frequent, for example:

– a daily update notice, on a dedicated website or notice-board first thing every morning

– on-site briefings – very short meetings, as required, to discuss and confirm plans

» clear and simple – notices should be in plain English, short and to the point.

ASK

Interview an experienced construction worker, with some level of supervisory responsibility, to find out more about teamwork among workers on-site. Work out your questions before you arrange the interview and ask your teacher to check these first.

You could ask:

✳ How do you get people who have never worked together before to work as a team?

✳ Why is teamwork so important on-site?

Keep notes of your questions and the answers given in the interview. Prepare a short talk based on the interview and present this to your learning group.

LINKS

Construction team roles

Jobs within a construction team fall into one or more of the following categories:

» operative   » supervisory and administrative

» craft and trade   » professional

» technical   » managerial.

The architect, for instance, has professional and technical expertise but can also be part of the management team for a project. Similarly the site foreman, who has a supervisory role could be a trained craftsperson. The team members and their roles and responsibilities are as follows.

The client
The client may take an active role or delegate all or some of the decisions to a contractor. The client usually selects the team members, by appointment or by **tender**. Team members may be selected based on a variety of criteria, such as:

» reputation, expertise and quality of work

» local to the area, therefore good for the local economy

» worked with other members of the team before

» price.

The architect
The architect must first consult very closely with the client regarding the design of the project, and then make sure that all aspects of the design brief are communicated effectively to all members of the team. For many large projects there will be a scale model to demonstrate the finished structure. Throughout the construction phase, the architect will:

» consult with all team members on the fine detail of the design and specifications

» assist with problem solving as issues arise.

Consulting engineer
The consulting engineer will clarify specifications with the client, architect, surveyor and building contractor to make sure that all the details are correct, suitable and understood by the team members.

The specifications may be modified as the consulting engineer collects data on-site. The consulting engineer will oversee the work on-site, consulting with the project or site manager and all members of the construction team.

Architectural technologist

The architectural technologist works on-site more than the architect, working with team members on the development of the project. The technologist will gather information about particular design issues and communicate the findings to the team, assisting with problem solving as necessary.

The information gathering could include:

» clarifying the client's preferences on details of the design

» researching: legal requirements relating to the design, selection of materials

» feedback from the client and stakeholders on:

- the progress of the project

- the quality and suitability of the final structure.

Project manager

Also called the site manager, the project manager is responsible for making sure that the construction team 'pulls together' and the project is completed safely within the planned timeframe and budget. The responsibilities include:

» liaising with all team members

» planning work schedules

» supervising site preparation

» briefing the workforce

» monitoring progress

» reporting to the client.

Estimator

The estimator works out the cost of the project, including materials, equipment, transport and labour. The project may be divided into components which can be tendered out. For example the client may invite tenders for the plumbing component, or the electrical component of the project. The estimator works out the specifications for the tender, consulting with other team members such as the buyer, surveyor and project manager. When the tenders come in they are compared to the estimator's costing.

Safety officer

The site health and safety officer has a supervisory role and is responsible for making sure that all site safety requirements are met. The safety officer communicates with all site personnel about specific precautions and safety rules and checks that these are followed. If an accident occurs, the safety officer conducts an investigation to find the cause and will make changes to safety procedures to ensure it doesn't happen again.

Surveyor

The surveyor's role is a technical one, similar to that of a quality checker. The surveyor makes detailed inspections of the project at various stages and reports the findings to the project team. The aim of the inspections is to:

» check that the construction is structurally sound

» identify defects, faults and quality issues

» ensure compliance with building regulations, fire safety requirements, accessibility specifications, sustainability standards, other quality standards specified by the client.

Where problems are identified, the surveyor will work through the issues with the relevant team members to ensure a suitable solution is identified.

Clerk of works

Also known as a site inspector, the clerk of works has a supervisory role ensuring that the work on-site is completed to specifications and will also keep records on site activities and events including:

» regular site personnel – numbers and job titles

» site visitors

» deliveries

» documentation received, such as drawings, specifications, instructions, especially where changes have been made to the original plan.

Craftspeople

Craftspeople usually work within their own team on large projects. The team leader will interact with the main construction team, to clarify design, planning, materials and other information. Each member of the craft team is responsible for:

» ensuring that work is completed to the required standards, including safety and quality

» reporting any issues, problems or faults:

  – this is very important; the solution to any problems that arise must be suitable for the whole project, not just one section.

Sub-contractors

The sub-contractors are brought in to perform specific components of the work, for example a plumbing or electrical sub-contractor. Contractors should be included in team notices, briefings and other communications and should also be committed to the goals of the project and to open communication regarding mistakes, faults, breakdowns and other issues.

Ask your supervisor at your work experience placement to help you to find out:

» what new methods of construction are used in the workplace and why were these introduced?

» what new construction materials have been introduced recently – and what are the benefits of these?

I want to be...

...an estimator

» **What documents and drawings do you use to work out what materials and resources are needed for a construction job?**

On most tenders we are issued with the employer's requirements which generally comprise the following: the contract for the works, preliminary items, drawings (either detailed or conceptual), NBS specifications for the works (such as brickwork ,roofing, timber, groundworks etc) – these specs give the levels of workmanship required and the types of material. We will also be issued with detailed specifications and other relevant information.

» **What materials can you usually get locally?**

Materials that can be got local to the particular project will be largely coincidental – for example, there might be a local quarry or brick works, or some materials may be sourced from demolition sites in the area. But most materials will have to be transported to a greater or lesser degree.

» **What sustainable materials do you know about?**

We tend to use recycled materials if possible. So, for a brownfield site we would try to use crushed concrete or brickwork produced on site for aggregates and bulk fills. Timbers are always from sustainable sources.

» **Do modern methods of construction save time and money? How?**

Yes, we would endeavour to use framed systems which do not rely on wet trades. Rather we would use lightweight steel metsec sections to form a base for facades which would be in steel or aluminium cladding systems. Superstructures could be framed in steel which has a time advantage over in-situ concrete. Factory-made bathroom and shower pods improve the site installation periods for finishes but may incur a premium on cost.

» **Do modern methods of construction reduce the level of risk on-site? How?**

Yes. More prefabrication means less requirement for working at height. Standards of safety on site are simply much better now. Scaffolds are safer, sites are tidier etc.

» **What can make material costs 'blow out' on a project? How can this be avoided?**

High levels of wastage have a massive effect on costs. This can be avoided by making subcontractors liable for the cost of their own waste – this ensures they will control it better. You could also implement a site waste management plan.

* Richard Graves

Site Visit

Primrose Hill →

The Wates Group were contracted to build 48 flats and 31 terraced houses for Yorkshire Community Housing. The client expressed the following preferences in their brief:

» the use of Modern Methods of Construction (MMC) – especially off-site manufacturing

» that the homes should achieve an **EcoHomes** rating of 'excellent'

» removal of wasteful elements of work

» consistent quality control.

The Wates Group consider that the cost of MMC techniques is generally higher than traditional methods but the benefits are:

» relief of pressure on-site

» a high level of quality control

» positive impact on issues such as health and safety, sustainability and quality.

The solutions chosen for the project were a timber frame for the houses and the Structherm Fast Build System for the circular three-storey flats. Some of the benefits of using these solutions were:

» speed of build – ten weeks' construction of 48 units on three floors

» excellent **'u' values**

» 15 per cent better than minimum standards required by building regulations

» clean and safe operation

» use of timber from renewable sources

» both systems compliant with render finish and timber cladding

» cost-effective.

FIGURE 4.7 **Primrose Hill Project**

Adapted from:

http://www.wates.co.uk/living_space/living_space_projects/primrose_hill/

Questions

» Find out about the Structherm Fast Build System by visiting the website:

http://www.structherm.co.uk/fastBuild.asp

Describe the Structherm Fast Build System in your own words.

» How long would it take to build the 48 units using traditional methods of construction?

» What is a 'u' value?

» How can a project receive an EcoHomes rating of 'excellent'?

Assessment Tips

The assessment for this unit is by external examination. You can prepare for this by making notes on the following topics and discussing your notes with your teacher and other learners:

Sustainability:

» What is sustainability? Write your own definition.

» How are sustainable timber products produced?

Plant and equipment:

» List all the types of large plant used on a construction site.

» What small plant is used on a construction site?

» What regulations cover the safe use of plant and machinery?

Materials and components:

» Make a list of materials and components used in construction and include at least one use for each item on the list.

» What is the raw material used to produce the materials you have listed?

» Which materials are used to form the walls of houses?

» How do construction drawings show which materials are to be used, and where?

Job roles in construction:

» How many people are employed in the construction industry?

» List the job roles of people working on construction sites under the following headings: Technical, Professional, Administrative, Operative, Craft.

» What are the main activities associated with each job?

» What are the main steps of a construction project – and in what order are they completed?

Have you included:

- A definition of sustainability and information about sustainable materials. ☐
- A list of plant and equipment used in construction and information about regulations covering their use. ☐
- A list of materials used in construction and details about their production and uses. ☐
- Details of job roles in construction. ☐

SUMMARY / SKILLS CHECK

» Modern construction methods and materials

✓ Modern construction methods and materials arise from the constant quest for better ways to do things. Innovations include the use of machinery (plant), modern construction techniques and new materials.

✓ Plant used in the construction industry includes: compactors, compressed-air equipment, plant for transporting material, plant for trench digging and excavation, piling rigs, plant for lifting and moving materials, concrete pumps, plant for access to work at heights and mobile lighting towers for night work. Plant and equipment make work much easier and efficient, but one disadvantage of mechanisation is hand-arm vibration syndrome (HAVS).

✓ Modern methods of construction (MMC) include all new methods of construction that speed up the construction process while improving safety, quality and environmental impact, such as off-site manufacturing and assembly – volumetric construction ('pods') and panelised construction. Other new methods include tunnelform, slab-deck and thin-joint block work.

✓ New materials are being invented all the time; these are lighter and stronger with better insulation qualities.

» Use of sustainable techniques

✓ Sustainable construction techniques and materials include energy conservation and sustainable building design, such as: passive solar heat and light, solar, wind or geothermal energy sources, renewable energy technology such as biofuels, better insulation and high-quality distribution systems, locally-sourced and sustainable materials, improved site and resource management, waste management, reclamation and recycling and the use of brownfield sites.

✓ Construction materials are sustainable if they are made from natural and renewable raw materials using low energy manufacturing processes.

✓ When selecting material for sustainability and efficiency, you should consider: the impact of sourcing and production on the natural environment, transport impacts, renewability, the lifespan or life cycle of the product, productivity, the effective use of energy and material and minimising wastage.

» Who works in the construction industry?

✓ There are 2,000,000+ people working in the UK construction industry.

✓ Teamwork is vital – people need to co-operate to ensure success.

OVERVIEW

The construction industry is important to all of us. Structures are essential for human environments – providing home and shelter; places for work, education, recreation, shopping and health support; roads and rail for travel; and essential infrastructure services such as water and power supply.

It's important that buildings and structures provide a healthy and pleasant environment for the community. The design and use of the built environment has a large impact on communities' well-being. The best designs provide a feeling of safety and security, and by showing respect for the community in the design, gain the respect of the community in the continued use and care of the structures. For example, if people enjoy the environments they live in, they are less likely to damage or deface them by breaking windows or daubing them with graffiti.

The construction careers in the usage stage of the lifecycle of a building include looking after the leasing and continuing use of buildings; ensuring that the needs of the occupants are met, monitoring the use and condition of buildings and structures and ensuring that they are well-maintained. Maintenance job roles include plumbers, electrical technicians and building service engineers.

Sustainable maintenance practices ensure that a structure has minimal impact on the natural environment throughout its useful life. Any major corrective maintenance work on a building will have an environmental impact. Planned preventive maintenance (PPM) should prevent the need for major corrective maintenance work.

05

Value and Use of the Built Environment

Skills list

At the end of this unit, you should:

» understand the basic function and use of structures

» understand how the built environment provides a feeling of society and wellbeing

» know how the built environment is maintained

» understand the job roles, career opportunities and progression routes, and the importance of teamwork, for those who value and maintain the built environment.

Job watch

Job roles involved in the value and use of the built environment include:

» estates officer
» facilities manager
» land and property valuer
» auctioneer
» building services engineer
» gas service technician
» electrical engineering technician
» plumber.

The function and use of structures

A structure must resist the forces that threaten to undermine its stability. These forces include gravity, ground movement, loads, high winds and other natural forces such as earthquakes. Structures have to stand up to:

» dead loads – the loads of the materials that form part of its structure

» live loads – the furniture and people within the building when it is in use, and natural forces from wind, soil movement and damp.

Buildings are designed and built to structural forms that are known to perform well. You can see which forms work by looking around at buildings that have stayed up for a long time – in some cases for hundreds of years. You can see what materials and which structural arrangements withstand the test of time. Research and testing of materials continually informs this process.

Structures have a variety of uses. Every built environment has an infrastructure of roads, railways, reservoirs, bridges and tunnels that provide the linking of services such as communications, goods, water and electricity to residential, industrial, public and commercial developments.

The visual and social impact of structures

The built environment has a mix of old and new structures. When you look around you can see a visual record of our cultural identity. Buildings from different eras reflect the taste and values of the social groups that existed at that time. The design and care of every structure gives us information about the people who designed, built, inhabited and preserved (or condemned) the built environment. For example, Victorian buildings, such as workhouses, congregational halls, public bars, public baths give us an idea about society as it existed at that time. You can also see how functions of buildings change over time. That Victorian workhouse, for instance, might have become a school in the 20th century, and has now been converted into expensive flats.

FIND OUT

See if you can identify two older buildings in your local area that have undergone a change of use since they were built. What sort of things do you think would have to be done to those buildings to make them suitable for their new role?

» street widening

» provision and maintenance of car parks in town centres and shopping areas

» improved street lighting and CCTV

» traffic calming methods – such as roundabouts and speed bumps

» creation of more green spaces in town centres

» providing local facilities such as libraries and sports centres

» improving access to buildings for people with disabilities

» making sure public transport reaches all areas

» bus lanes to improve public transport services

» providing cycling routes.

FIGURE 5.4 **Good planning can make the built environment a pleasant place to live and work**

The built environment, employment and economic opportunities

About two million people work in the construction industry and the industry provides work for about a million more in:

» extracting materials used by the industry

» manufacturing construction supplies

» providing services used by the industry.

Most jobs in construction and construction-related industries are well paid. These wages and salaries are used to buy property, goods and services in the area, creating a cash flow into other parts of the economy. Industrial and commercial buildings that are thoughtfully planned, designed and created by the construction industry attract new businesses to move in and set up in an area. Good design and high-quality construction may attract businesses from other parts of the country, and even overseas. As more high-profile businesses are attracted to an area, more jobs become available, more money is paid to workers from the local community and the economy thrives. This is good for the local community and the nation as a whole. The profile of the area is lifted within the business community and it becomes a 'happening place'.

Another economic factor is the ongoing value of each building. Most buildings have increased re-sale value due to the continuing rise in property prices. Buildings that have been well planned, designed and built will increase in value at a higher rate than inferior buildings. Good construction is a good investment.

FIGURE 5.5 **How many people do you think were employed in the building of the new Wembley Stadium?**

Consider one commercial or industrial building that you know quite well. Think about all the ways in which this building has created employment and wealth. These questions may help you:

✱ What business is conducted in the building?

✱ How many people are employed there?

✱ What sort of work do they do?

✱ Who looks after the building? Include cleaning, security and maintenance jobs.

✱ Who constructed the building? How many people would have been employed to do this – in what job roles? Include surveyors, building inspectors, architects, craftspeople.

✱ Who made the components and fittings used in the building – such as pods, roof trusses, panels, heating system components, electricity and water supply components?

✱ Who mined and treated the raw source substances required to make the materials and components used in the building?

Prepare and present a short talk about the employment and wealth created by your chosen building over the construction and use phases of its life cycle. Use labelled photographs or sketches, tables and text or a PowerPoint presentation to illustrate your talk.

LINKS

How the built environment is maintained

Sustainable buildings are designed with ongoing maintenance needs in mind. Ideally the amount of maintenance required will be minimal. Any replacement materials, components and fittings should be easy to source locally – reducing energy and transport impacts; and produced using sustainable technologies.

Design for sustainable maintenance

Design features that enable sustainable maintenance include those that:

» minimise adverse impacts on the environment

» protect and enhance the diversity of nature

» use energy, water and other natural resources efficiently

» minimise waste and re-use or recycle materials wherever possible

» encourage the use of the least environmentally damaging forms of movement and transport

» incorporate habitats for wildlife.

Reduce emissions

Almost half of the carbon emissions in the UK come from energy use in buildings. Sustainable design must reduce the **carbon footprint** of structures. The carbon footprint is the total amount of greenhouse gases emitted over the full life cycle of a building. Incorporating energy efficient systems into the design will ensure that the ongoing maintenance of the building keeps carbon emissions to a minimum. These design features may include the use of passive solar heat and effective insulation.

Reduce waste

Sustainable design should also make provisions for sustainable waste management throughout the life cycle of the building

Reduce potable water usage

Potable water is water suitable for drinking. **Grey water** is the waste water from washing your hands, taking showers and washing the dishes. This grey water can be used to flush the toilet and water the garden. Design features for the sustainable maintenance of a building should include large waste-water storage and rainwater collection tanks and a grey-water delivery system to toilet cisterns and irrigation systems.

Long-lasting and economical

Design for minimum maintenance reduces the environmental impact and the operating costs of the use of the building. Designs should include strong and long-lasting structural forms and materials and the use of external coatings that provide a high level of protection from weathering and wear and tear.

Reduce transport pollution

Locating buildings close to public transport will reduce the need for individual car journeys. This is a sustainable design and maintenance feature and a good selling point since car fuel and

FIGURE 5.6 **Habitats for wildlife are considered in designs for the built environment**

Deconstruction

When they came to the end of their useful life, buildings used to be demolished – knocked down and the waste and rubble thrown away. Now they are 'deconstructed'. This means taking out any re-usable parts gradually and carefully. Salvageable items can include windows and doors, fireplaces, fixtures and fittings, roof tiles and even the bricks themselves. Although it is almost always preferable to straight demolition, deconstruction still has an impact on the environment, including:

» pollution – noise, dust and exhaust fumes from actual deconstruction work, transport to, from and around the site and from the use of plant and equipment

» energy consumption

» possible toxic products used in the original construction of the building, such as asbestos and lead.

CHECK IT OUT

This website includes a list of 'dos and don'ts' in maintaining an old building.

http://freespace.virgin.net/mp.hearth/Directory.html#anchor871645

FIGURE 5.8 **Deconstruction of a building – many of the components can be re-used rather than thrown away**

Careers in valuing and maintaining the built environment

Once a building is completed it is handed over to the owner and occupants to use. At this stage, the roles of people involved in the construction industry change – and there are new roles in building management and valuation. The building must be looked after properly in order to maintain its value.

Professional roles

There are job roles specific to managing and valuing real estate. Here are some examples, with weblinks to professional bodies that support these roles.

Estates officer or manager

People in this job manage the land and property belonging to wealthy families or organisations such as local councils or health authorities. The work involves the management of leasing, letting, sales and tenants, and organising maintenance and repairs. For this work you need a degree or professional qualification, for instance in technical or chartered surveying.

Facilities manager

A facilities manager (or site manager) manages the use and maintenance of the building once it is complete. The work involves making the best use of space and arranging and managing refurbishment, renovations, upkeep, maintenance of the structure and contents, cleaning, waste disposal, catering, parking and security.

Most facilities managers have a foundation degree, BTEC HND or degree in facilities management or a qualification in management, business studies or chartered surveying.

Land and property valuer or auctioneer

This job involves working out the market value of real estate including land, buildings and commercial property. It is usually a specialisation moved into by people qualified as surveyors. You need a degree or professional qualification approved by the Royal Institution for Chartered Surveyors (RICS) to become a land and property valuer.

CHECK IT OUT

Find out more about this work from the Royal Institution of Chartered Surveyors (RICS)
http://www.rics.org

CHECK IT OUT

Find out more about this role from the British Institute of Facilities Management (BIFM)
http://www.bifm.org.uk

CHECK IT OUT

Find out more about this work from the Royal Institution of Chartered Surveyors (RICS)
http://www.rics.org or the National Association of Valuers and Auctioneers
www.nava.org.uk or http://www.naea.co.uk/qualifications/careers5.asp

Craft and technical specialisations

People in different types of construction career can specialise in valuing and maintaining the built environment. The initial training will be the same, but specialist training may be required, for example in heritage restoration. Here are a few examples.

Building services engineer

In this area, a building services engineer oversees inspection and maintenance programmes for services such as water, gas and electricity supplies, lighting, heating and air-conditioning, telecommunications, security systems, and lifts and escalators.

Gas service technician

This job involves maintaining and repairing gas appliances and systems such as gas meters, fires, boilers and cookers, central heating systems and shower units. The work includes maintenance checks, testing controls and safety devices, fixing gas leaks and faults, and replacing worn parts.

To get into this work you need an NVQ in Domestic Natural Gas Installation and Maintenance or equivalent qualification, and ACS and CORGI registration. You may be able to get into this job through an apprenticeship scheme or move into the role from other work such as engineering, building services engineering or plumbing.

Electrical engineering technician

For building maintenance, the work of an electrical engineering technician involves maintaining and repairing lighting, heating, air conditioning, lifts and escalators. It includes inspecting and testing electrical installations and machinery to make sure they are working correctly and safely, and drawing up preventive maintenance rotas. You may be able to get into this job through an apprenticeship scheme or complete:

» BTEC Certificate/Diploma in Operations and Maintenance

» BTEC National Certificate/Diploma in Electrical Engineering

» City & Guilds Progression Award in Electrical and Electronics Servicing (6958) Levels 2 and 3

» City & Guilds Certificate in Electrotechnical Technology (2330) Levels 2 and 3.

CHECK IT OUT

Find out more about this occupation from the Chartered Institution of Building Services Engineers (CIBSE)
http://www.cibse.org

CHECK IT OUT

Find out more about this work from The Council for Registered Gas Installers (CORGI)
http://www.trustcorgi.com

CHECK IT OUT

Find out about this work from Science, Engineering and Manufacturing Technologies Alliance (SEMTA)
http://www.semta.org.uk

Plumber

The plumber services and repairs fittings and equipment for hot and cold water supplies, heating and cooling systems, drainage networks, weatherproofing, roofs and guttering. Some plumbers specialise in sheet-metal work, for example on historical buildings.

Find out about one maintenance task performed regularly by workers in your chosen sector of the construction industry.

What sustainable principles apply to the methods and materials used in performing this task?

MANAGE

Conduct a case study of an historic building in your local area. Ask your teacher to help you to identify a suitable building and contact people who would be willing to help you with your research.

Make sure that your case study covers the answers to the following questions:

✻ When was the building constructed?

✻ Who was the architect?

✻ Is the building heritage listed?

✻ Why is the building important to the local community?

✻ What major alterations or additions have been made to the building since it was first constructed? List the dates and details of the work.

✻ Have there been any major restoration works? What did these involve?

✻ Who is involved in the ongoing maintenance of the building and what do each of these people do to ensure that the building is kept in good condition?

Create a report on your case study including:

✻ a description of the building outlining its:
  – history in brief
  – current use
  – importance to the community

✻ tables – listing, for example:
  – dates and details of significant alterations and additions
  – the people involved in maintenance and upkeep and details of their roles

✻ photographs of the building labelled to show, for example:
  – later additions to the structure
  – current maintenance work.

LINKS

...a facilities manager

» What buildings do you manage?

Three large London offices.
Regional Offices – Manchester, Leeds, Cardiff, Bristol and Birmingham

» What sorts of things do you need to think about when you plan the use of space inside a building?

Number of staff to be housed
Network requirements
DDA requirements
Fire regulations
Health & safety issues
Maintenance
Nature of working being carried out

» What areas or rooms need refurbishing or renovating most frequently? Why?

Areas which all staff use regularly. For example kitchen/restaurant areas. Meeting rooms, reception areas and toilets. These areas are used on a daily basis by all staff so therefore have a lot of traffic going through them causing wear and tear.

» How do you keep track of the wear and tear on the building and the maintenance needs?

Regular inspections.

» Who do you employ to do the building maintenance and repairs? Could you describe which parts of the building each person maintains?

Dalkia Maintenance is the contracted maintenance company. We have two on-site engineers who work in the building full-time. They look after all the mechanical and electrical areas (air-conditioning, boilers, etc) along with all reactive maintenance (blocked loos, broken doors, etc).

» What requirements do you have in your buildings for cleaning, waste disposal, catering and parking? How do you organise people to supply these services?

Cleaning – Contracted cleaners, three daytime cleaners and 20+ night-time cleaners.

Waste Disposal – London Recycling collect normal waste as well as all in-house recycling (paper, plastic, etc.).

Catering – Contracted catering, 23 staff on-site manage our in-house restaurant.

Parking – No parking is available for staff, however one bay is kept for disabled visitors. We have a loading bay for deliveries.

❋ Anita Sewell

Site Visit

Railway nursery – BBC Action Network →

The BBC Action Network runs a programme about people who take action to save buildings in their community. One project involved a derelict ticket and parcels office built in 1915 at Whitstable railway station and closed in the early 1980s. The locals decided it would be perfect as a new site for their nursery.

The building is in a conservation area, but not listed. It was boarded up, damp and vandalised with holes in the floor and no ceiling.

The community contacted the Railway Heritage Trust about their idea of restoring the building and putting it to good use. The Trust was very supportive and after a lot of hard work and negotiation the project also gained funding for the restoration project from Network Rail who still owned the building. The Welsh slate roof alone cost £96,000 to restore. The work also involved replacing or restoring sash windows, old fireplaces and sliding doors.

The community funded the fitting out of the restored building as a nursery themselves. They installed toilets, a kitchen, partition walls and full disabled access. The nursery opened in September 2005. Find out more about this project at
http://www.bbc.co.uk/dna/actionnetwork/A13240342]

FIGURE 5.9 **The railway nursery before redevelopment**

Questions

1. Why do you think this building had fallen into such a poor state of repair?

2. What is a 'conservation area' and why are some buildings in such an area listed, and some not?

3. What is a sash window? Where could you find suitable sash windows for this building?

4. What recommendations would you make for the ongoing sustainable maintenance of this building?

Task One: Report on the design of a simple structure You will be given a design for a simple structure. Make some notes on the following to support your research and reporting assessment task on the:

» proposed site for the project – including photographs

» suitability of the design for the intended purpose and use

  – think about the human needs identified in this chapter

  – how would you expect these to be met?

» the effects of the structure on the community and local properties – for example:

  – does the structure fit in with the character of the area?

  – will the structure reduce the amount of green space in the area?

  – will there be any increase in the volume of traffic or pressure on car-parking spaces?

» effects on the natural environment:

  – is the site greenfield or brownfield?

  – is there any loss of wildlife habitat – if so, how can this be compensated for in the design?

  – what sustainable design and maintenance features will help to protect the environment?

In addition, you should include information on the ways that changes to the built environment can improve the health, safety, security, social integration and general well-being of the community. For example: improved street lighting and CCTV, traffic calming methods, creation of more green spaces.

Task Two: Advertise jobs in the value and use of the built environment Your advertisement could be posters and leaflets, a recording for a radio promotional feature, a video recording for a television promotional feature, or a website.

Review the job roles listed here and on the Teacher Resource Disk and make notes on information to be included in your advertisement.

The information should include:

» a list of the jobs and careers available

» details of each job role – making it sound as interesting as possible!

» the relevant professional institutions.

 E - p o r t f o l i o

Create a Word file for your notes and insert a header and footer. Put your name, candidate number, centre name and centre number in the header and use the page numbering feature in the footer. Sketches should be no larger than A3 and should be included in your evidence portfolio.

Have you included:

Notes on human needs that should be considered in the design process ☐

How buildings and structures contribute to community well-being, including fitting in with local characteristics and protecting the natural environment ☐

How sustainable maintenance principles can be built into a design ☐

Details of careers in the value and use of the built environment. ☐

SUMMARY / SKILLS CHECK

» The function and use of structures

✓ A structure must resist forces such as gravity, ground movement, loads, high winds and other natural forces such as earthquakes. Some structural forms have lasted for hundreds of years and show what materials and which structural arrangements withstand the test of time. The mix of old and new structures around us are a visual record of our cultural identity; some older structures are recognised as important historical records and given protection. The life cycle of a building starts when it is originally constructed. During its useful life, many changes may occur and finally the building is deconstructed or demolished. The majority of structures have a finite life cycle and are replaced after a period of time.

✓ Since the first Planning Act, over sixty years ago, planners allocate land for different purposes. There is currently a shortage of land for housing. Different types of land use include: private housing development, public buildings, public spaces, agricultural, commercial and industrial, transport infrastructure, utility infrastructure, government institutions, religious usage and leisure and tourism.

» How the built environment provides a feeling of society and well-being

✓ People want safe, clean, friendly and prosperous places in which to live and work with good amenities such as shopping and green spaces. If people feel respected and consulted, and find that their needs are met by the built environment, the environment will be cared for and the people living in it will be content.

✓ The construction industry makes an enormous contribution to society, providing the physical environment for human activities. Features of the built environment are planned to have a positive effect on the health and well-being of the population, and minimal impact on the natural environment. Planning legislation encourages improvements to the built environment that will regenerate urban areas and improve health, safety and security.

✓ About two million people work in the construction industry itself, and construction provides work for about a million more in extracting materials used by the industry and in manufacturing construction supplies and providing services.

✓ Industrial and commercial buildings that are thoughtfully planned, designed and created by the construction industry attract new businesses to move in and set up in an area.

» How the built environment is maintained

✓ Sustainable buildings are designed with ongoing maintenance needs in mind. Ideally the amount of maintenance required will be minimal. Sustainable principles in design that allow for sustainable maintenance include: reducing emissions, waste, transport pollution and potable water usage; making sure the structure is long-lasting and economical; and incorporating habitats for wildlife.

✓ Any major corrective maintenance work on a building will have an environmental impact. Preventive maintenance should be regular enough to prevent the need for major corrective maintenance work. Replacement systems, fittings and components should comply with current standards and have a high sustainability rating.

» Careers in valuing and maintaining the built environment

✓ Once a building is completed the roles of people involved in the construction industry, especially in craft areas, change to a maintenance and repair role. There are also new roles, for example estates officers, facilities managers and valuers or auctioneers. Many of these job roles have professional associations that look after their members' interests, inform about new developments in the industry and promote training and skills.

OVERVIEW

Different types of buildings and structures require different maintenance approaches – some are subject to more wear and tear, such as schools; others to severe weather conditions. However, all buildings require some looking after, even those protected from harsh environments and frequent use. The designer should select materials and components to suit the use, performance requirements and life expectancy of the structure. These should stand up to the expected wear and tear on the building if Planned Preventive Maintenance (PPM) is conducted regularly. PPM involves work that prevents any significant damage to the structure – for example, renewing paint and varnish finishes on walls and timber to prevent the damage that can be caused by damp penetration. The costs of maintenance should be worked out as part of the construction planning and costing procedures. High-quality work and timely repairs will reduce maintenance costs.

Once completed, and in use, a building must be inspected regularly and any maintenance and repairs required should be recorded. Plans should be drawn up to ensure repairs are completed in a timely, but logical way. Common defects or problems that you find in most buildings include: flaking paintwork, damaged door fittings, dripping taps, leaking pipes, damp and problems with electrical fittings. If major repairs are necessary, these must be planned carefully and scheduled in consultation with the owner and occupiers of the building.

As with all construction work, maintenance tasks must be carried out in accordance with health and safety requirements – these include using the correct PPE, access equipment and manual-handling techniques. You need to develop safe working practices for performing maintenance tasks and review these regularly to identify and incorporate improvements to the quality and safety of your work.

06

Maintenance of the Built Environment

Skills list

At the end of this unit, you should:

» know the factors influencing the engagement of stakeholders and the whole community in the development and use of the built environment

» understand the social, economic and commercial contribution of the built environment to the wider community

» be able to analyse job roles, qualifications and career progression opportunities, and the importance of teamwork, in asset management, use and maintenance of the built environment.

Job watch

Job roles involved in maintenance include:

» plumber

» carpenter

» electrician

» building services engineer

» facilities manager

» home inspector

» building control officer

» building surveyor

» quantity surveyor.

Good design and quality work means less maintenance

Building designers must consider all the factors that could affect a building's survival – then select and specify materials that will withstand these factors, using British Standards as guidelines. Construction materials are tested by their manufacturers under extreme conditions to ensure they comply with British Standards. For example, in an area exposed to severe weather, wind-driven rain can saturate walls, which may then be liable to frost damage. The specifications for a building in this location may **stipulate** that frost-resistant bricks are laid in a 1:4 cement:sand mortar ratio to withstand the weathering effects. Specifications may also require that the quality of work is in accordance with standards such as BS 8000 'Workmanship on building sites'. If good design and workmanship are lacking a building may fail to fulfil its function properly. A badly designed building will require far more repair and maintenance than a well-designed one.

What is maintenance all about?

Even when a building is designed and built well, it will still need maintenance to make sure it continues to withstand potentially damaging conditions, both inside and outside. Ideally maintenance should be carried out regularly to a pre-planned schedule. Maintenance carried out in this way is called 'Planned Preventive Maintenance' (PPM). The key concept of PPM is that prevention is more economical than repair.

Maintenance costs
The client funds both the construction costs and operating costs of a building. Operating costs are usually about five times more than the construction costs.

Operating costs are calculated by a quantity surveyor, and depending on the type and use of the building, they can include:

» heating

» lighting

» hot and cold water services

» waste-water bills

» mechanical services, such as lifts

» fire alarms

» access security

» intrusion alarms

» air-conditioning

» cleaning costs.

Internal maintenance

Internally, a building is subject to:

» wear and tear on the floor, surface and wall finishes

» products with a finite lifespan stopping working – for example light bulbs

» mechanical parts becoming worn – for example working parts in a lift

» accidental damage – this could apply to any part of the building

» condensation, damp or leaks – these may affect decorative finishes, damage electrical surfaces or even result in inhospitable conditions for inhabitants.

FIGURE 6.1 **Accidental damage to a building has to be allowed for in maintenance plans and costing**

External maintenance

Externally, a building is subject to:

» the effects of the weather – for example: wind, extremes of temperature, rain and damp

» atmospheric and environmental conditions, such as pollution – for example traffic exhaust fumes can leave carbon deposits on limestone.

How can you extend the lifespan of a building?

Good design and quality of work can extend the life of a building. Some examples of this include:

» painting or rendering masonry where required, especially external walls – this reduces the **porosity** of the masonry, helping to prevent damage by penetrating damp

» ensuring that all exposed timber, such as doors and window and door frames, are coated with paint or varnish – this will prolong the life of the timber

» sealing door and window frames with silicon sealant – this will keep openings watertight and draught free

» keeping gutters free from leaves and debris to avoid blockage – a blockage may lead to storm-water overflow and potential dampness down a face or area of the building

» making sure brackets to drainpipes are secure

» periodically checking drainage inspection chambers and rodding them when required

» repointing defective pointing on masonry – this saves expensive repairs being needed later

» re-pointing flashings – this will prevent damp from soaking down the chimney stack and affecting interior walls

» repairing defective plaster or render

» injecting a silicon-based damp-proof layer where damp-proofing has failed or where it was never installed

» replacing loose roof tiles and re-roofing when required

Dripping tap

Tap washers provide a seal between tap and seating. Most new washers are made from rubber – very old ones are made from leather. These eventually wear thin or perish, due to hardness of water in some areas or just due to time.

If washers are not replaced regularly, the seating of the tap – made from brass, phosphorous bronze or cast alloy – may also wear prematurely and cause drips leading to leaks.

Defective plaster

May be caused by damp penetration from substrate or condensation on surface leading to blowing or lifting of plaster from wall.

Water and damp penetration

This could be caused by:

» cracked or slipped roof tiles or slates

» leaking pipework – under floors, in loft spaces, above ceilings or from fitting joints

» poorly fitting windows and doors, especially attic roof windows – this is sometimes caused by shrinkage of the timber in the frame

» defective gutters – faults could include: an inadequate join at the fitting between lengths or where lengths join downpipes; blockages; an overflow that leaks on to a wall – eventually the wall will become saturated, and in the worst cases fungus or moss can appear, or the mortar may wash out and the masonry will become loose

» inadequate or failing damp-proof course (DPC) or cavity tray over lintels in cavity

» materials, such as rubbish and garden waste, stacked against walls causing a build up of moisture

» vegetation encroaching above the DPC level

» wall ties with mortar droppings acting as bridge for moisture in the cavity

» condensation build-up due to poor ventilation

» lack of pointing at sheet weathering and roof flashings – if the pointing fails there is no barrier against damp at critical locations on the building, such as verges where roofs or walls abut, or where chimneys join the roof line – then rain will penetrate and soak down into interior walls.

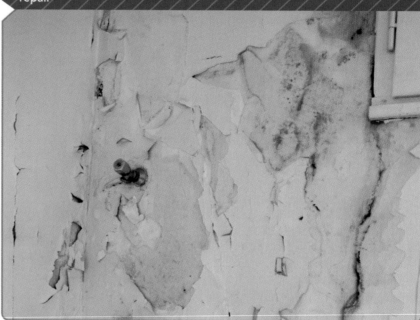

FIGURE 6.4 **Penetrating damp is a sign of damage or a defect needing repair**

CHECK IT OUT

For more information about timber problems visit the DIYData and DIY Doctor websites:

http://www.diydata.com/problem/timberrot/timberrot.php

http://www.diydoctor.org.uk/projects/dry_rot.htm

Timber decay and infestation

Unprotected timber leads to problems such as rotten floorboards or window frames. These may be caused by:

» dry rot – a fungus found in moist unventilated conditions, and which can destroy structural timbers, skirting boards, door frames and wood flooring – it looks a bit like cotton wool

» wet rot – timber becomes 'spongy' – this is usually caused by structural or paint defects leading to high moisture levels in the timber. You can check for rot by pushing a thin-bladed knife into the timber frames – it should stop after a short distance.

Refer also to water and damp penetration, above.

Faulty electrical fittings and equipment

Problems may include:

» fittings not being flush with the background wall or ceiling, etc. – if there is a gap there may be a potential for electrocution – for example, a child may prod the gap with thin metal object

» fittings out of alignment – for example, not level or plumb.

JOINING IN

Conduct an inspection of your own home, or of another building that you have easy access to. Check for any signs of the defects mentioned in this section and note down:

the visual signs of each defect or problem

the cause of the problem.

Take photographs or draw sketches to show the where the problems are.

Fill in a checklist to ensure that you have checked every aspect of the building that may require maintenance.

For example:

Check for:	Note findings:	Note cause:
Poor work quality		
Flaking paintwork		
Cracked windows		
Damaged door fittings		
Dripping taps		

L I N K S

Keep your completed table in your e-portfolio with the relevant photographs. Discuss your findings with your teacher and ask for feedback on your assessment of the probable cause of the problems. Change your notes in the table if necessary.

Preparing a Planned Preventive Maintenance schedule

A Planned Preventive Maintenance (PPM) schedule may be prepared by the company that owns the building or by specialist contractors.

To prepare a schedule you need to:

» identify what needs doing – this information could come from:

  – fault reports from users

  – manufacturers' recommendations

» work out when each job needs to be done – this involves:

  – prioritising tasks – which are the most urgent?

  – working out whether one job needs to be done before another can be started – for example fixing a leak before repairing the walls or floors affected by the leak

  – schedule inspection timings across a year.

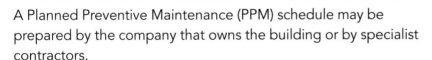

DID YOU KNOW?

From the 14th December 2007, every home that is sold in the UK is required to have a Home Information Pack (HIP), which includes a Home Energy Rating. Home Inspectors will provide a Home Condition Report and Energy Performance Certificate. Find out more about HIPs by visiting the website:

http://www.home informationpacks.gov.uk/industry/

The timings for inspections and actual maintenance work may be scheduled on an annual, three-monthly, monthly or weekly basis. For instance, a boiler may require a full service annually with an interim lighter check and service every three months. Motors for mechanical lifts may need a three-month service, whereas filters and pumps may need more regular monthly checks and services.

For large buildings or estates, the PPM schedule is computerised, using a specialist software program.

Health and safety

Maintenance schedules save expenditure on costly repairs and also help reduce health and safety risks. Here are two common examples.

1. Logging the temperatures for the circulated water in air-conditioning systems as part of PPM schedules helps to prevent Legionnaires' disease – a flu-like illness that can be fatal. It is caused by *Legionella* bacteria that thrive in water temperatures of 25–45°C.

2. Replacing fluorescent lights that are flickering. These pose a risk for people prone to seizures caused by the flickering. When bulbs have reached the end of their life cycle, power is wasted by heating the electrodes in the appliance instead of providing light.

CHECK IT OUT

The Stratford-on-Avon District Council website gives details of service checks to help prevent Legionnaires' disease.

http://www.stratford.gov.uk/community/community-384.cfm

CHECK IT OUT

Look at the costings for maintenance work on public buildings and schools in the London Borough of Barking and Dagenham on this website:

http://www.barking-dagenham.gov.uk/7-ed-policy-adm/ed-admn-asset/pdf/schedule-of-rates.pdf

FIGURE 6.4 **Example of a PPM schedule for a two-storey building**

Asset Code, Description, Floor, Location and category	Year-Week:	2007-32	2007-33	2007-34	2007-35	2007-36	2007-37	2007-38	2007-39	2007-40	2007-41	2007-42	2007-43	2007-44	2007-45	2007-46	2007-47	2007-48	2007-49	2007-50	2007-51	2007-52	2007-53	2008-01	2008-02	2008-03	2008-04	2008-05	2008-06
231785-AIR1003-001|WC Extract Fans - Packaged Unit|SUB-Plant Room - ROUT																	6M												
231785-AIR1003-002|WC Supply Air Fan and Filters|SUB-Plant Room - ROUT																	6M												
231785-AIR1101-001|Executive Toilet Supply Fan No 1|9TH-AHU Plant Room - ROUT		1M				1M			1M					3M					1M				1M					6M
231785-AIR1101-002|Boiler Room Supply Fan No 1|BASE-Basement Boiler Room - ROUT							1M			3M			1M				1M			6M				1M				
231785-AIR1101-003|Boiler Room Supply Fan No 2|BASE-Basement Boiler Room - ROUT							1M			3M			1M				1M			6M				1M				
231785-AIR1102-001|Kitchen Theatre Extract|9TH-AHU Plant Room - ROUT		1M					3M			1M				1M				6M				1M						1M
231785-AIR1102-002|Calorifier Room Extract Fan|SUB-Plant Room - ROUT							3M			1M			1M				6M				1M			1M				
231785-BLG2301-001|Extension Ladder 3 Stage|ROOF-AHU Plant Room - ROUT											1Y																	
231785-BLG2301-002|Clamp Meter Digital|BASE-Office - ROUT											1Y																	
231785-BLG2301-003|Multimeter|BASE-Office - ROUT											1Y																	
231785-BLG2301-004|Temperature Reader|BASE-Office - ROUT																												
231785-BLG2301-005|Step Ladders|BASE-Store Room - ROUT											1Y																	
231785-BLR2101-001|Boiler No 1|BASE-Basement Boiler Room - ROUT			1Y																									
231785-BLR2101-002|Boiler No 2|BASE-Basement Boiler Room - ROUT			1Y																									
231785-BUR0201-001|Burner No 1|BASE-Basement Boiler Room - ROUT			1Y													3M												
231785-BUR0201-002|Burner No 2|BASE-Basement Boiler Room - ROUT			1Y													3M												
231785-CHI1301-001|Boiler Flue Fan No 1|ROOF-Roof - ROUT										1Y																		
231785-CHI1301-002|Boiler Flue Fan No 2|ROOF-Roof - ROUT										1Y																		

TEAMWORK

Work in a group with two or three other learners and draw up a PPM schedule for a simple two-storey building. Ask your teacher to help you to identify a suitable building to inspect. This could be your own home, part of your school or college or another simple structure. You will need access to the manufacturers' information on components such as heating and hot water systems.

You need to work as a team to:

* inspect the building

* examine the relevant documents

* identify defects

* list components requiring maintenance

* identify the causes of any faults

* list remedial work required to remedy faults.

Keep a record of:

* the material that you researched

* your notes on the building inspection

* your lists of defects, causes and remedial work required.

Draw up a schedule of when the work should be completed.

LINKS

Safe working practices

Look back at the Health and safety at work section of Unit 3. Remember you have a responsibility to co-operate with your employer on health and safety strategies and to take care of yourself, any other people that may be affected by what you do, and any equipment you use. This includes:

» following company procedures and work instructions

» using the personal protective clothing and equipment (PPE) required for specific jobs

» working safely, using safe work methods

» using, storing and maintaining tools and equipment correctly

» being aware of hazards and risks, and taking recommended measures to avoid these.

Follow health and safety regulations

Under the Health and Safety at Work etc. Act 1974 (HASAWA) both the employer and the employee have responsibilities. Your responsibilities include being aware of hazards and following procedures, such as using the correct PPE and safe work methods. Employers should 'take all steps, as far a reasonably practical, to ensure your health, safety and welfare at work'.

The Work at Heights Regulations have specific requirements for young people working under supervision, these are to:

» report safety hazards to your employer or supervisor

» use all the equipment and safety devices properly and follow the procedures demonstrated in your training or instructions.

If you think any equipment or the procedures are unsafe, consult your employer or supervisor.

Pay full attention to all health, safety and welfare training. Ask as many questions as you need to, until you feel confident to do your work safely. Take up the opportunity for more health, safety and welfare training whenever you can.

Use the correct PPE for the job

Remind yourself of the various types of personal protective equipment you may be required to use by referring back to Unit 3. In addition to the equipment listed there you may also have reason to use:

» a respirator with a built-in filter to provide protection from heavy dust

Always keep PPE in good condition:

– keep it clean

– check 'use-by' dates

– inspect for cracks, dents and tears

– report faulty or out-of-date equipment.

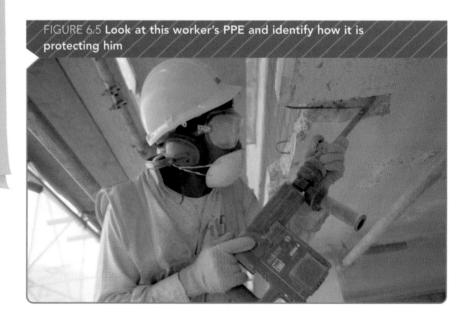

FIGURE 6.5 **Look at this worker's PPE and identify how it is protecting him**

» a positive air respirator for use in situations where the air has toxic contaminants, such as asbestos dust

» rubber gloves, to protect from long-term exposure to water

» heat-resistant gloves, for working with hot metal

» chemical-resistant gloves, for protection from acid burns

» sunscreen, to protect from skin cancer

» a broad-brimmed hat to prevent sunburn.

MANAGE

Select three maintenance tasks that could be required in a two-storey building that is over 20 years old. Ask your teacher to check your selections.

✱ Use the Internet, look through relevant textbooks on maintenance or consult experienced professionals to find out how the work should be done.

✱ Research the work steps required to perform each of the three maintenance tasks chosen and the PPE that you should use to perform each step.

✱ Note down the tasks, steps and PPE required for each of the three jobs.

Keep your notes in your e-portfolio, Discuss the steps for each job, and the PPE selected with your teacher and make any corrections necessary. Give a short presentation to the class on one of the maintenance tasks.

LINKS

Use access equipment safely

Refer again to the section in Unit 3 on working at height. Hazards include:

» ladders placed too far from work

» fragile roofs

» weight of materials on scaffold too heavy

» guard rails or other edge protection missing.

Risk-control measures for avoiding falls from heights should always be implemented. They include:

» using a scissor lift – this is a small vehicle with a safe platform with guard-rails and toe bars that can be raised to different heights. A safety harness attaching the worker to the lift must be worn

» using a scaffold – a structure built using metal pipes and boards by a qualified scaffolder. Ensure that:

- scaffold tubes are plumb and level

- there are base plates or timber sole plates on uprights

- scaffold or platform is secured to the building

- platforms are fully boarded

- there is edge protection on platforms

- scaffold is be accessed from a secure ladder

- using mobile elevating work platforms for fragile roofs, where possible; be sure that the plant operator is trained and competent

» using ladders only for short tasks involving no heavy work. You should:

- check that the ladder is in good condition

- secure it at a 75 degree angle, with at least two rungs above the resting height

- never over-reach from a ladder – get down and move the ladder closer to the work.

FIGURE 6.6 **Well-constructed scaffolding helps to ensure worker safety**

Before a permit is issued to work on a roof, the authorising officer will check that:

» risk assessments for the particular site and job have been made

» fall protection from edges, ladders, scaffolds or through fragile materials is in place

» equipment for prevention of falls (such as harnesses) is available and in good condition

» workers have received all relevant training

» communication systems are in place (such as a two-way radio).

Use safe manual-handling techniques

Safe manual handling covers methods for pushing, pulling, lifting and lowering loads. There are safe manual-handling techniques for every different type of job. Handling loads incorrectly can cause severe or permanent back injury, so each time you learn a new task make sure you learn any new manual-handling techniques associated with it. You should never attempt to move a load weighing more than 20–25kg by yourself. Materials should be ordered in, or transferred into, 20–25kg bags.

You should receive manual-handling training and be provided with equipment, such as trolleys or sack trucks, for lifting and moving heavy objects and materials.

For example, the procedures for manually laying a block wall could include:

» using blocks of less than 20 kilos

» having the blocks placed as near as possible to the work and on a flat surface

» using gloves, safety boots and a safety helmet

» making sure the blocks do not have to be lifted above shoulder height.

Look back at Unit 3 to remind yourself of the steps for safe manual handling.

CHECK IT OUT

Find out more about working at height problems and solutions by visiting the web community on the Health and Safety at Work website:

http://webcommunities.hse.gov.uk/inovem/inovem.ti/WorkAtHeightSolutions/groupHome

Consider all your practical experience of conducting maintenance tasks. Reflect on the methods used and the health and safety precautions taken. Can you identify any changes resulting from your increasing experience? Your observations could range from finding it easier and quicker to put on and adjust PPE so that it fits correctly, to finding better ways to complete tasks – for example, having materials closer at hand.

Discuss your safe work practices with your learning groups and teacher. What can you learn from other students or from experienced maintenance staff at your work placement?

Keep notes in your e-portfolio on safe work practices and improvements you have made to your methods and safety.

LINKS

Ask your employer and experienced colleagues at your work placement about any special maintenance tasks that they may have conducted, such as removal of asbestos or lead.

Find out what safe work methods are used in these special circumstances.

» estimated costs including the hire of equipment or specialist services

» disposal of waste.

Review your practical experience of maintenance tasks and the activities, websites and examples in this chapter to refresh your knowledge of common repairs and their associated causes, methods, materials, costs and health and safety issues.

Keep notes on this information in your e-portfolio.

Activity C. Review this chapter and make notes on the ways that good design, good quality of work and Planned Preventive Maintenance can prolong the life of a building and reduce operating costs. You should include:

» selecting materials and components to suit the environment and use of the building

» examples of the results of poor work quality and notes on how the problems could have been avoided

» the cost benefits of Planned Preventive Maintenance.

Task Two: Applying safe working practices to a routine practical maintenance activity

You will be asked to conduct a common maintenance task such as:

» changing a tap washer

» replacing a door lock

» re-pointing brickwork

» replacing a faulty electrical fitting.

Prepare for this assessment by:

» reviewing your notes on continuous improvement of your own safe working practices

» asking the advice of experienced professionals

» practising these, and other similar maintenance tasks and asking for feedback on the quality of your work and the safety of your work methods.

Assessment Tips

Create a Word file for your notes and insert a header and footer. Put your name, candidate number, centre name and centre number in the header and use the page numbering feature in the footer.

Have you included:

A checklist of things to look for when inspecting a building. ☐

Notes on common repairs and the associated causes, methods, materials, costs and health and safety issues. ☐

Notes on the benefits of good design, quality work and planned maintenance. ☐

Notes from your personal reflection activity on improvements to your safe working methods. ☐

SUMMARY / SKILLS CHECK

» Good design and quality work means less maintenance

✔ Good design and quality of work can extend the life of a building. Building designers consider everything that could affect the lifespan of a building and select materials that will withstand these factors. However, even the highest quality building will need maintenance to withstand internal and external wear. Planned Preventive Maintenance should ideally be carried out periodically to a pre-determined schedule – prevention is more economical than repair. The timings for inspections and actual maintenance work may be scheduled on an annual, three-monthly, monthly or weekly basis. Maintenance schedules save expenditure on costly repairs and also help prevent health and safety risks.

» Common building and structural defects

✔ You need to be able to recognise the earliest signs of defects and fix problems before they progress into a major repair job. Make sure you find the cause of each defect. Common defects include: poor quality work, flaking paintwork, cracked windows, damaged door fittings, rotten floorboards, dripping taps, defective plaster, water and damp penetration, timber decay and infestation, sheet weathering and faulty electrical fittings and equipment.

» Safe working practices

✔ You have a responsibility to co-operate with your employer on health and safety strategies – for example being aware of hazards and following procedures, such as using the correct PPE and safe work methods. Keep PPE in good condition: keep it clean; inspect for cracks, dents and tears; check 'use-by' dates and report faulty or out-of-date equipment and replace as necessary.

✔ Falls from height cause half of all the fatal accidents on construction sites. Risk-control measures for avoiding falls from heights include using a scissor lift, scaffold or mobile elevating work platform.

✔ Safe manual handling covers methods for pushing, pulling, lifting and lowering loads – each time you learn a new task make sure you learn any new manual handling techniques associated with the task.

OVERVIEW

Construction methods used in the past were developed using whatever materials were available locally, such as timber and stone. They relied on craft skills perfected over hundreds of years and hard physical labour – there were no mechanical aids or power tools around! Simple buildings would take weeks or months to complete; complex structures, such as churches, could take decades. For example – it took 74 years to build Liverpool Cathedral, which was constructed using local sandstone and oak.

Today, the pace of life and the size of the population has increased dramatically so that modern buildings must be constructed much more quickly, using efficient and sustainable materials and methods. The objectives in modern construction are to reduce the time and cost of construction while increasing quality, safety and sustainability.

How can this be achieved? Over the last 50 years or so, new technology and materials and more mechanisation have resulted in new methods of construction. Innovations include: sustainable design incorporating strength and aesthetics; light, strong, durable, and recycled materials and safer physical construction techniques. These include off-site assembly and the increased mechanisation of physical tasks. Research and innovation continue in the construction industry, with new materials and methods being formulated, tried and tested daily.

These new methods must offer benefits in speed, quality, cost and sustainability.

The timelines for construction projects are planned using Gantt charts which show:

» the different tasks that have to be done

» which of these can occur at the same time

» which ones have to be scheduled after some other preparatory work

» how long each task and stage should take.

providing warmth inside. In houses built before cavity walling, the most common thickness for external walling was nine inches and was laid in what is known as Flemish bond. The façade of the building would be built in the best-quality bricks, known as facings, while the sides and rear would more often be built with bricks of a lesser quality, called commons.

Strong, durable bricks with low porosity, known as **engineering bricks**, were previously extensively used for bridges, tunnels and sewers. Reinforced concrete has largely replaced this usage.

Cavity walls

The use of cavity walls began to replace solid masonry walls in the early 20th century. The principle of a cavity between two leaves of masonry still dominates the design of the majority of habitable buildings today. The air space created by the cavity acts as a barrier to damp penetration and the cavity slows thermal transfer, particularly when the cavity is insulated, for example with polystyrene. This ensures that buildings are better at staying warm in cold weather and keeping cooler in hot weather.

Stone

Stone has been used for construction for centuries, with buildings constructed from whatever stone was locally available. For instance you get flint used a lot in the south and southeast, limestone in the Cotswolds, Derbyshire and Yorkshire and slate in Wales and the Lake District.

Slate

Slate is a durable stone found in parts of England and Wales. It has been used in building for centuries. Because it breaks cleanly along very flat surfaces it has found a particular use for roofing tiles and paving slabs. It is also **impervious**, making it useful as a damp-proof course laid just above ground level on walls in buildings. It can also be used to construct fireplace surrounds and hearths.

Slag blocks

These black blocks were commonly used in 18th-century buildings. They were manufactured from waste material produced when copper ore was smelted – an early example of waste recycling! The sizes were similar to blocks used today. The blocks were waterproof and used for footings, cellar walls, quoins and semi-elliptical copings on outside garden walls.

Lath and plaster walling

A lath is a thin strip of material – usually timber. Laths were nailed to timber studs or ceiling joists, with narrow gaps left in between the horizontal strips for the plaster to grip. Traditional plaster mortars are mixtures of sand, lime and water – these were applied with a plasterer's trowel. The plaster squeezed through the gaps in the laths and provided a backing for later coats of plaster. Horse or goat hair was added into the mix to help prevent the plaster from cracking as it cures.

Multi-coat plaster finishes

Plaster finishes are built up in coats of different mixes and thicknesses. For example, three-coat work involves:

» the first 'backing' coat – also known as a rendering, pricking-up or scratch coat – this should ideally be 10 to 15mm and definitely no more than 20mm thick

» the second 'floating' coat – again 10 to 15mm thick – this provides an even surface for the last coat

» the 'finishing' coat – applied as a smooth surface between 3 and 6mm thick.

Three-coat work is typically used for timber lath or expanded metal lath backgrounds. Two-coat work has only the floating and finishing coats and is used for masonry backgrounds. External render coats are built up in a similar way although the finish coat is often float-finished to achieve a suitable background for paint finishes. Alternatively a roughcast finish, which gives a textured appearance, may be used.

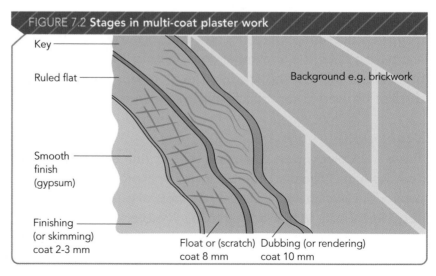

FIGURE 7.2 **Stages in multi-coat plaster work**

Key

Ruled flat

Background e.g. brickwork

Smooth finish (gypsum)

Finishing (or skimming) coat 2-3 mm

Float or (scratch) coat 8 mm

Dubbing (or rendering) coat 10 mm

Fixed partitioning

Partition walls are internal walls that divide rooms within a building. They may be: load bearing – helping to support walls, floors or other structural elements; or non-load bearing – providing a way to divide up space – giving privacy and a barrier to sound and thermal loss.

Partition walls are constructed using:

» brickwork or blockwork built off the foundation or floor slab and carrying on up through the building

» stud partition walls – upright timbers nailed or screwed to horizontal supports, which start fixed at floor level and provide a frame for lath-and-plaster or plasterboard.

Solder-type copper fittings

Copper fittings are fairly lightweight, versatile and inexpensive. Various diameters can be shaped to perform a range of functions in internal domestic pipework such as hot and cold water supplies and heating. First-fix pipework is ducted through the carcass, for example under floors or behind walls. The plumber returns for a second fix to connect appliances, such as boilers and sanitary-ware after the walls and floors are in place. The fittings are soldered to the pipes with a flux that is heated by a blowtorch until it melts and seals the joint.

ASK

Find out which traditional methods of construction are still used in your selected sector of the construction industry. Ask your teacher to help you to identify and contact experienced construction workers who would be willing to talk to you about traditional methods of construction. Prepare your questions carefully beforehand, for example:

✱ Which traditional methods of construction do you still use on modern buildings?

✱ Which traditional method do you think requires the most skills and experience?

✱ Which traditional methods of construction have been largely replaced in modern buildings?

✱ What special traditional skills would you need to restore an historic building?

Note the results of your research in your e-portfolio. Discuss your findings with your teacher and other learners exploring the advantages and disadvantages of the traditional methods that you learned about. Keep the notes of your discussions.

LINKS

What new methods do we use now?

While traditional methods of construction are still used, some methods are being replaced by new techniques. Some of these are described below.

Pre-fabricated buildings and structures

Pre-fabricated buildings and structures are typically used for temporary offices or site facilities due to their ease of portability (they can be machine-loaded onto low-loaders and transported). They are modular – that is they are manufactured in rectangular shapes that can be built up as required, and accept extensions should the need for expansion occur. Factory-controlled manufacture ensures the interior fittings, fixtures and layouts can be made to various designs depending on the end use.

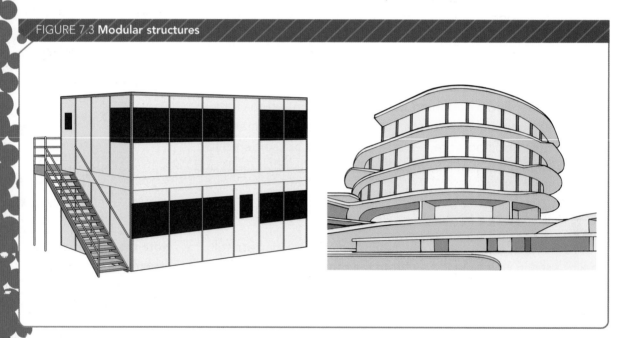

FIGURE 7.3 **Modular structures**

Steel- or timber-frame buildings

Steel-frame buildings are suitable for commercial, agricultural or industrial purposes. The walls and roofs of the portal frame structure can be covered with plastic or metal cladding, cement sheeting, or composite panels.

Timber-frame buildings are becoming more popular in the private house building sector of the construction industry. The off-site construction of frames reduces error and fewer site inspections are required. The fast erection of the frame by crane leads to much quicker weatherproofing of the structural envelope.

Plasterboards

Plasterboards are 1200mm-wide sheets of gypsum sandwiched between two layers of paper – usually recycled. These are used for partitioning and wall surfacing. They can be fixed to masonry walls with dabs of plaster or nailed using flat-headed plasterboard nails or screwed onto studs at 600mm centres. The joints where boards abut each other can be taped and painted directly, or scrim tape used to cover the crack, and the board given a skim coat of gypsum plaster as a finish.

Dry lining

Dry-lining systems are a fast method of partitioning spaces and can be erected using timber or metal stud partitions with boards of various composites fixed on, for example plasterboard. The board finishes are specified according to the requirements for acoustic and thermal properties and decorative finish. Some dry-lining systems are load bearing and used on a variety of structures, ranging from residential buildings to commercial projects. Specialist tradespersons fit both the studwork frames and the boards: dryliners make the walls, tackers fix the ceilings.

Curtain walling

Curtain walling is a frame fixed to the main structure that clads the external skin of a building. Modern curtain-walling systems are metal frames that are fixed, usually at floor level, and infilled with panels of any suitable material – glass is a popular choice. Curtain walls have the advantage of being lightweight and space-efficient; they can be assembled on-site and craned into position. They provide a fast method of enclosing the structure and have the bonus of not involving wet trades (such as bricklaying) in erecting and/or finishing the external skin.

Thermal blocks

These are lightweight concrete blocks with excellent thermal efficiency properties, also known as aircrete blocks and manufactured from pulverised fuel ash (PFA), lime, sand and aluminium powder. They are widely used on the inner leaf of a cavity wall to limit heat loss from inside to out.

These blocks are load bearing and can be used anywhere in a structure. They are increasingly used below ground level in the footings on buildings to improve thermal efficiency.

CHECK IT OUT

Find out more about dry-lining systems from the drywall manual on the Lafarge Plasterboard website:

http://www.lafargeplasterboard.co.uk/drywall_manual/default.html

DID YOU KNOW?

The 'wet trades' include trowel occupations and painters – both trades leave a trail of work that needs a drying-out period. Factoring this into a building programme slows down the speed of the construction. Eliminating or reducing wet trades from the schedule allows a dry working environment for mechanical and engineering services to be fitted.

Although thermal blocks are used in a similar way to brick and blockwork construction there have been developments in their application that now put them in the MMC category.

These are:

» the use of blocks that are 610 x 215mm – this is larger than the regular 440 x 215mm size of block and results in faster building of blockwork

» the use of thin-joint blockwork systems:

– the first course is established as perfectly level using traditional mortar

– the blockwork is then laid onto a thin adhesive bed – only 3mm, compared to the traditional 10mm nominal thickness

– the adhesive sets much quicker than traditional mortars thus speeding the construction rate of the job.

The blocks can also be bought in even larger sizes, leading to even faster construction.

Push-fit plumbing fittings

Plastic pipe is easy to fit and can be used in place of copper pipes for carrying water through cold and hot water supplies. Plastic piping is pre-moulded but some types can also be bent to go round gentle curves. Most plastic pipe is connected by push-fitting connections. The fitting is simply pushed directly onto the pipe where it clicks firmly on, giving a watertight joint. These are also used for copper-to-copper and copper-to-plastic connections. Plastic-to-copper connections are not suitable for connecting directly to boilers as the heat may cause the plastic pipe to melt.

Using push-fit joints removes the need to use blowtorches, flux, solder and wire wool (necessary for joining copper fittings). Push-fit plumbing fittings are expensive, but the speed and ease of fitting often justifies their purchase.

CHECK IT OUT

For more information about thermal blocks visit the following websites:

http://celcon.co.uk/index.php?do=Page&pid=118

http://www.aircrete.co.uk/pdfs/factsheet4.pdf

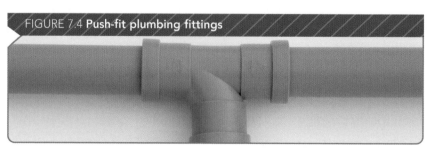

FIGURE 7.4 **Push-fit plumbing fittings**

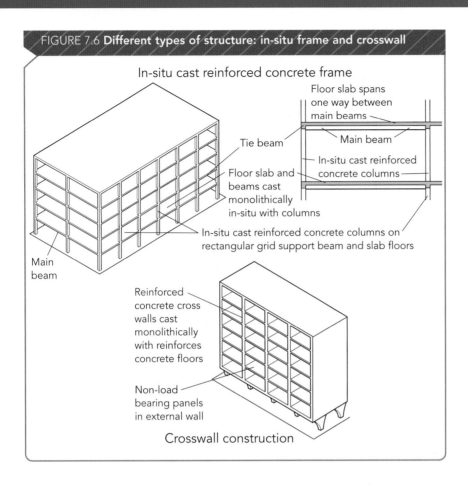

FIGURE 7.6 **Different types of structure: in-situ frame and crosswall**

In-situ cast reinforced concrete frame

Floor slab spans one way between main beams

Main beam

In-situ cast reinforced concrete columns

Tie beam

Floor slab and beams cast monolithically in-situ with columns

In-situ cast reinforced concrete columns on rectangular grid support beam and slab floors

Main beam

Reinforced concrete cross walls cast monolithically with reinforces concrete floors

Non-load bearing panels in external wall

Crosswall construction

Speed, quality, cost and sustainability

It is quicker and easier to assemble components in a factory rather than on-site because of the ability to create production lines. For example, a wheel-mounted platform can be rolled into a static position, the brickwork built, the panel rolled out and machine lifted onto lorries ready for transportation and machine unloading at the site.

Any on-site construction activity that can be streamlined affects speed, quality, cost and sustainability. For example, mortar is traditionally mixed on-site in cement mixers, poured into wheelbarrows and distributed in buckets onto the bricklayer's spot board by the labourers. This is very time consuming and requires many operational stages. Alternatively, a cement-mixing lorry can deliver daily batches to the site, which are then poured into large tubs and machine lifted to accessible positions. This speeds productivity, provides a consistent mortar, reduces labour costs and – because less transportation of materials takes place (cement and sand being delivered in bags) – saves fuel and thus contributes to sustainability. The use of silos that produce mortars on-site also has this effect. Obviously, due to economies of scale this example only works when the site is large; on a smaller site it may be more cost-effective to produce mortar in small mixers, or even by hand.

Why are speed, quality, cost and sustainability important?

For property developers and business owners, time is money. Many clients demand that their design requirements are met not only to tight budgets but also on time. Financial penalties are imposed on contractors that do not complete projects according to the timescales agreed in the contract.

The construction industry is a major player in society's move towards sustainable development. MMC offer economic, social and environmental benefits such as:

» quality control during manufacture
- this ensures that there are fewer defects and potentially saves costs in rectifying errors and defects caused by weather or poor work quality

» safer work environment
- factory work is safer – sites are inherently hazardous; factory work is also more stable and the workforce stays longer in one place – site-work employment can be insecure due to its temporary nature

» reduced waste, reduced transport and the use of energy efficient materials all have environmental benefits.

In situ construction methods

Certain structural elements can be formed in situ. In situ means making it in the position it remains in. Concrete, which can be cast into almost any shape anywhere, is a case in point and is used in situ for foundations, floor slabs, under kerbstones and lintels.

Masonry walling is also constructed in situ. Brick and block walls are built in situ whereas concrete is cast in situ.

An interesting new method uses lightweight insulated blocks that act as permanent formwork for concrete to be poured in situ. The blocks are interlocking and require no mortar or similar bedding material. The finished walling is strong and thermally efficient.

Off-site construction methods

Off-site methods can have cost and sustainability benefits. Here are some examples.

Trussed rafters

The traditional method of roof construction involves the assembly of roof trusses on-site by carpenters. Deliveries of timber have to be stored and then nailed and screwed in situ – the trusses are built on the roof space itself.

More frequently nowadays, timber trussed rafters are pre-assembled off-site using graded timber joined into triangular shapes by steel nailplates. These can be delivered at the time they are needed on-site and lifted by crane directly onto the structure. Carpenters then fix the trusses to the wallplate.

Timber-frame construction

Although timber-framed buildings can be assembled on-site, they also lend themselves well to off-site assembly. Increasingly, this is the case. The frame is delivered to the site on lorries and crane-lifted into position. The frame is secured to the concrete foundation by bolting a sole plate into position. Vertical wall studs form a frame structure that is stiffened by the plywood sheet cladding as well as the joists that form the floors and the trusses that form the roof. There are usually cavity walls that may have an external leaf of weatherboard timber sheeting or masonry that is connected to the inner leaf. A vapour barrier and insulation fill the cavity.

Structural steel frames

A frame is like the skeleton of a structure – many modern structures are steel framed. Steel has high strength and is an excellent material for providing a load-bearing structural frame. These can be manufactured off-site and clad in a range of materials internally and externally. In many circumstance steel has to be given a fire-resistant coating such as cement or plaster. This is because steel will fail quickly in the event of a fire if unprotected.

> ### CHECK IT OUT
>
> Find out more about timber-frame construction by visiting this website:
>
> http://www.timber-frame.org/html/understanding-the-issues/multistorey-construction/?PHPSESSID=36cae5e0d2776920a6c6a

Erection techniques

Satisfactory erection of structures begins with accurate setting out by the site engineer. Next, the groundworkers excavate trenches according to the determined lines and pour concrete, which forms the foundations. In traditional construction the bricklayers then erect masonry walls from the footings to wallplate height, building gables at ends of roofs where necessary. Once above head height the brickwork is taken up in stages, known as 'lifts'. The scaffold determines each lift height. The scaffold can be either a putlog type that partly relies on the structure for support, or an independent scaffold that is free standing.

Independent scaffolds can be erected before the superstructure (the structure above ground floor level) is built. This method is often used when timber-frame buildings are crane-lifted into position. Cranes may be positioned on-site for the entirety of the build or hired as needed (due to high running costs).

Cranes also aid in lifting:

» steel tubular poles and fittings for scaffold construction

» heavy components such as lintels, sills, steels and mortar tubs

» timber roof trusses

» palletised items such as bricks, blocks and roofing tiles.

Steel-frame structures can be assembled on-site using a combination of crane assisted positioning and fixing by means of mobile elevated working platforms that allow access at height for the steel fixers.

The scaffold has a designated bay for the crane to load materials onto. Hoists may also be used to transport materials vertically to the working area.

FIGURE 7.7: **Materials are delivered to a designated area**

THINK

Consider the following two methods for building a garden shed:

1. Erecting a pre-fabricated shed

   You can buy 'packs' of pre-fabricated shed wall, floor and roof panels which are delivered to your home. You can put these together yourself – or pay extra and have the staff build them for you. One example is the 1st Choice Leisure Building company's 'Malvern/Bewdley' shed, featured on the following website:

   http://www.leisurebuildings.com/malvern/bewdley-garden-sheds.html

2. Build a shed from recycled materials

   You can use old timber or corrugated iron to erect a shed to your own design. One example is a shed made from old warehouse pallets featured on the following 'Self-sufficient' website:

   http://www.self-sufficient.co.uk/Build-a-Pallet-Shed.htm

   What are the advantages and disadvantages of each method?

   Think about the following aspects of the construction methods:

   * time   * sustainability

   * safety   * cost

LINKS

Make notes about the two different methods, and your views on the advantages and disadvantages of each one. Keep these notes in your e-portfolio.

Discuss your views with your teacher and other students. Keep notes on any new ideas from the discussion in your e-portfolio.

Working schedules

Programme charts, known as Gantt charts, are used on-site to plan and monitor the progress of work. They are drawn up by Head Office and used on a daily basis by the site manager to check that site activities are running according to plan. The chart details labour and site processes. Materials, plant and equipment are utilised according to the schedule.

FIGURE 7.8 A simple construction Gantt chart

Ridgewood Construction PLC

Month	One	Two	Three	Four	Five	Six	Seven	Eight	Nine	Ten	Actual Completion
Set up site / Site Clearance											
Excavations											
Concrete Foundations											
Substructure Brickwork											
Concrete Ground Floor											
First Lift Brickwork											
Internal Partitions											

Since variables to the plan may occur – such as delays caused by the weather – planned and actual times of site activities are recorded on the chart in parallel rows below the timings columns. In this way the chart can be analysed on a daily or weekly basis to make adjustments to the schedule. Activities may be completed before predicted (planned) times, in which case there is an opportunity to advance operations, or if the work is behind schedule the planned timings of anticipated events may have to be re-scheduled.